TWO
NEIGHBORHOODS
IN HARLEM
[VOLUME 1]

TWO
NEIGHBORHOODS IN HARLEM
[VOLUME 1]

BURRELL SPEIGHTS

CITI OF BOOKS

CITIOFBOOKS, INC.
3736 Eubank NE Suite A1
Albuquerque, NM 87111-3579
www.citiofbooks.com
Hotline: 1 (877) 389-2759
Fax: 1 (505) 930-7244

Ordering Information:
Quantity sales. Special discounts are available on quantity purchases by corporations, associations, and others. For details, contact the publisher at the address above.

Printed in the United States of America.

 ISBN-13:   Softcover   978-1-960952-06-6

Library of Congress Control Number: 2022919509

Acknowledgments

I would like to extend a warm and special thank you to my father, mother, sisters, brother, nephews, niece, cousins, extended family, and friends.
I do not know what I would have done without the joy you all have provided me with.

Additionally, I would like to thank Barbara Cannella and William Katechis, who pitched in without a moment's hesitation by looking over my first few chapters and responding to my endless barrage of questions.

Foreword

I was more than thrilled when it occurred to me one day that I had enough stories to tell to make for a pretty good and interesting memoir. I knew that it would be enjoyable for not only adults, but because of the many life lessons therein, it would be good for young people to read too. Given all the time I have spent thinking of things to write about over the years, I do not know why the idea took so long to come to me to tell my story. Nevertheless, despite the delayed arrival of my idea, I was even more thrilled when I realized how much fun it would be for me to revisit so many people and places by writing about them. So with bells and whistles going off in my head, I immediately set aside another writing project and started this one.

From early on, one undeniable fact is that I have had the good fortune of being in the right places at the right times. Coupled with that good fortune, and with my curiosity being what it is, I almost always find myself trying to actively involve myself with anything that catches and holds my attention.

Thinking about the bits and pieces that make up my story was nothing new for me. Hardly a day has gone by without me thinking about at least one of the many funny, inconceivable, and even stressful events that were a part of bringing me to this present day. But when it occurred to me to write my story, I saw things from a different perspective. Rather than the usually disjointed, haphazard, and scattered perception of it all, I saw an orderly stream of events timed in a way that made them perfect to write about.

Being a story that I know all too well, I knew that there would be no storylines to come up with, outlines to construct, characters to name, dialogs to write, or any kind of time-consuming research to be done. So like the scattered pieces to a puzzle in my head for far too long, I knew that they all needed to be shaken loose, organized, and put into words.

As I thought more about how to approach the writing, I realized that the biggest tasks facing me would be reaching back into my trove of memories and then finding the words to tell this long story. But given the perfectly aligned sequence of events, I was sure that it would be a reasonably quick and easy writing project.

Even before typing my first word, I had a good sense of how to set everything up with my opening paragraph. Along with that, I saw how my story would unfold and how connected everything would be. But what I didn't know was how, when, or where to end it. Additionally, I didn't have it divided into titled chapters; all I had was one long narrative without an ending. Despite these missing pieces, I was not overly concerned; I enjoy absolutely everything about writing, especially the process of solving problems that inevitably come with the writing process.

In the end, it took me 11 months to complete my first draft, and it felt good to finish such a large writing project in this relatively short period of time (while holding down a full-time job). At that point, I knew that the only thing left for me to do would be to go back to the beginning to see what I had, and then smooth out any rough spots in the many pages of writing that I had compiled. With the meticulous care that I had given to this first draft, I was sure that it would take no more than one or two more drafts before I had a completed manuscript with well-titled chapters. But, as I discovered, it was really only the beginning, because my anticipated one or two drafts grew to a whopping total of 193. So now after 193 drafts that took almost 11 years, I think I have finally crafted a story that I would like to share with you, and I hope that you enjoy reading it half as much as I have enjoyed putting it together.

Visit the website to see photos and more: *twoneighborhoodsinharlem.com.*

Burrell.

Immersed in the Joy of Books:
A Transformative Experience at the Book Fair

I enjoyed being around so many people and children who so much enjoy books and reading. Seeing and reading their T-shirts expressing their love of books and watching them happily carrying their new books was such a thrill for me. It is an odd thing for me to say, but I honestly wish that I were like them. I do not dislike reading but it is something that I do not do as much as I would like. My mother used to tell me that I should read more all the time, and she was so right. I talked to one guy who came up from "the Valley" (I think that he meant Fresno or Modesto), but I got the clear impression that it was a long trip for him) and he was thrilled to be there. I also saw kids walking around with their noses buried in books too; and I always get a kick out of seeing that. I even found myself calling out to people of all ages and types passing by (who seemed unapproachable to me) to tell them about my book. While something that I do not do generally, I did it a lot yesterday. It felt very odd to do this, but it was fun for me at the same time; it felt as if I had transformed myself into another type of person. And once I got beyond the hard exterior to tell them my book's website address or to tell them to take a picture of my poster, it was smooth sailing with plenty of smiles, laughter, and good conversations. One woman told me that she loved reading and if she doesn't like my book that I would hear about it from her. But I was lucky enough to be able to tell her that I have not gotten one complaint after five years. I had to come out of my shell because it was a good opportunity to promote and talk to so many people. I talked to so many people that I could not even complete most of the songs that I played, so I did something like a medley of my song collection. Anyway, it was a lot of fun for me to spend a good 4-hours talking with these people who love books so much. So, I think I will be firing up the bat mobile to find some of these book fairs more often.

For Your
Reading Pleasure
two
Neighborhoods
in harlem.com

Read it to your sons
and daughters; and have your
daughters and sons read
it to you. The life-lessons,
laughs, and juicy words
were meant to have
a lasting impact on
EVERYONE.

Loaded
With: Adventure, Music,
Laughs, Suspense, Travel,
Flutes, History, People,
Culture, Education,
Storytelling, and more;
see how it compares
with your favorite book

A
Five-star
Ebook + Memoir

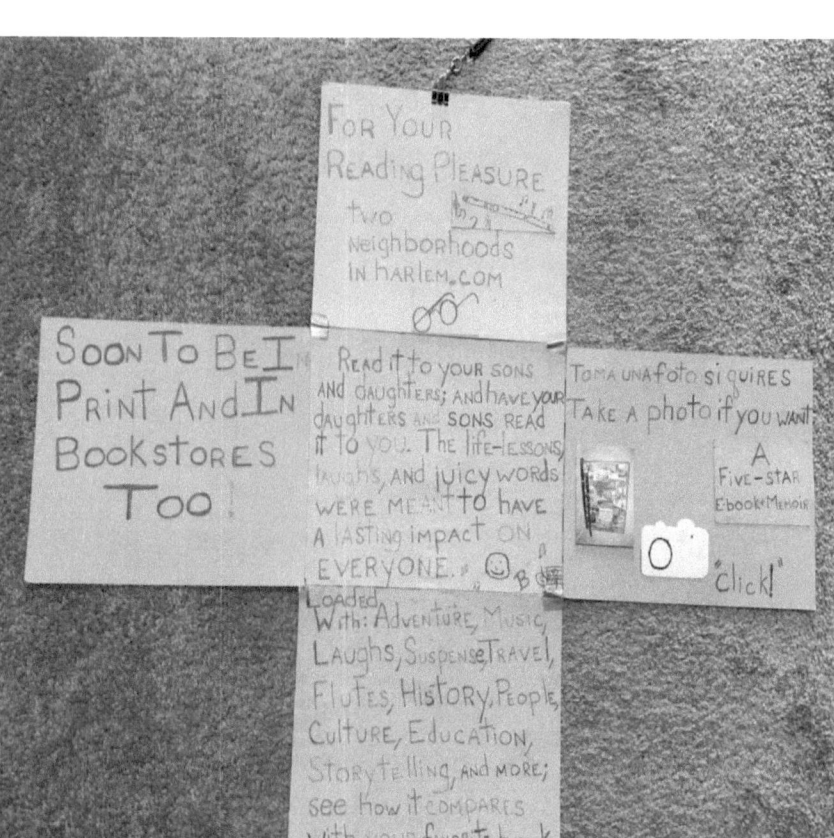

FOR YOUR
READING PLEASURE
Two
Neighborhoods
IN HARLEM.COM

SOON TO BE IN
PRINT AND IN
BOOKSTORES
TOO.

Read it to your sons
and daughters; and have your
daughters and sons read
it to you. The life-lessons,
laughs, and juicy words
WERE MEANT TO HAVE
A lasting impact ON
EVERYONE. ☺ B
Loaded
With: Adventure, Music,
Laughs, Suspense, Travel,
Flutes, History, People,
Culture, Education,
Storytelling, and more;
see how it compares
with your favorite book

Toma una foto si quires
Take a photo if you want

A
FIVE-STAR
Ebook+Memoir

"click!"

Contents

One Additional Backstory:

Before getting into this backstory, I would like to thank you kindly for picking up a copy of my book.

What you saw on the previous page are the first ten chapters of *"Two Neighborhoods In Harlem;"* but there are more. I would have loved to include all 30 chapters in this printed version, but it did not seem to me to be very practical. Being an unknown, self-published author without a literary agent or the support of a publishing house, I knew that trying to work my way through this very new and different world was not going to be easy. I also knew that the cost of printing so many pages would be exorbitant, thus ultimately making the retail price high too. From the beginning, publishing an affordable book has been something that was just as important to me as writing it. Like any other writer, I wanted my book to reach the hands of as many readers as possible. Even before I had finished writing it in 2018, and even now with a full 5-years of book-promoting in my rearview mirror, more than just a few people have made it clear to me that they are old-fashioned and that they enjoy the feel and even the smell of printed books. I have held plenty of books before and I have even gone as far as putting one up to my nose to see get a better sense of what they were talking about. But to me, it smelled like paper and felt like any other book that I have held. Nonetheless, who am I to question or quibble about other people's preferences, "to each his or her own," as the saying goes. Anyway, hearing this as much as I did, I knew that this printing-cost issue was going to be a problem for me that I had not thought about. But the solution I came up with was this: I would break the book down into three volumes. Since the book is comprised of 30 chapters, breaking the story down into 3 volumes seemed to be the way to go. It would enable me to reach lovers of printed books and keep the retail price low, too. So as I mentioned above, what you saw on *the previous page are the chap*ters of Volume I. But as a preview, I have included the chapter titles of Volumes II and III. So, take a look and see what you think:

VOLUME II

VOLUME III

VOLUME - I

1

Hamilton Heights
Is Where It All Started

Distraught, stunned, traumatized, displaced, despondent, and disoriented, I had no idea where I was or how I got there. It was as if someone had pulled a rug out from under me, and in a lot of ways, this was close to what had actually happened. My parents decided to move from our cozy neighborhood in Hamilton Heights without mentioning a word to me about it beforehand, and my small world had been turned completely upside down. The sudden change was like a body blow that had knocked the wind out of me. Even with the spectacular view of 125th Street, Manhattan's southeastern skyline, the Empire State Building, and the two popular streets that intersect in front of our new building, I was beyond being consoled.

Little did I know we were starting our lives anew in one of the most vibrant and culturally diverse neighborhoods in Harlem, if not the entire island of Manhattan. Our newly constructed high-rise was within walking distance to the Apollo Theater, Spanish Harlem, Grant's Tomb, the Julliard School of Music, the Jewish Theological Seminary, Harlem's Renaissance Ballroom, Riverside Park, the Barnard College for Women,

Teachers College, the Hudson River, the Schomburg Library, the (former) Cotton Club, Morningside Park, Big Wilt's Small Paradise, the Harlem Opera House, Columbia University, the City College of New York, and Riverside Church. Be that as it may, being only eight years old, I had no idea what this new neighborhood had to offer. Not only that, but the good things that come from living in such a culturally diverse community were well beyond the narrow scope of things that were important to me. All I could think of was what we had left behind.

Before moving to Morningside Heights, we lived twenty-six blocks to the north in a section of Harlem called Hamilton Heights. Hamilton Heights was named after Alexander Hamilton and distinguished residents of Hamilton Heights have included Lena Horne, George Gershwin, Count Basie, Norman Rockwell, Duke Ellington, and Roger Hammerstein.

I lived with my father, mother, twin sister, and younger brother. The original plan was to name my sister and me Gail and Gary. My parents never followed through with that plan, and chose the rather odd names of Vermell and Burrell for us; then for our younger brother, Reggie, they went with a more common name. We have another sister who was born by way of my mother's previous marriage, and she lived with her father in South Carolina. Her name is Doris, and she told me years later that our mother had no idea she was going to give birth to a set of twins before my sister and I were born. Then later, in the recovery room, when the nurse handed my sister to my mother, she told my mother that she would be bringing me to her shortly. This was when and how she learned that there were two of us, and her reply to this surprising bit of news was, "Oh my God!"

We lived on the top floor of a typical old-style New York City tenement walk-up that is probably much like the ones you may have seen plenty of times. Our apartment had two bedrooms, a living room, a kitchen, a slightly elevated bathroom floor (that I liked), a long hallway, a family room, a dumbwaiter (that we used for garbage), and a set of French doors led from our living room to our parent's bedroom. Our two living room windows were on the front side of the building, so we had a bird's-eye view of the row of apartment buildings across the street and the lively Harlem street scene five floors below. I can still hear the watermelon man as he rode his horse-drawn wagon down the middle of 151st Street chanting, "Waaaadeemeloooo," as people gathered to buy the fresh fruit he had for sale.

Near the northern end of Harlem, and adjacent to the historical Sugar Hill neighborhood, our apartment building was (and still is) in the middle of the block between Amsterdam Avenue and Broadway. I might add that it is the same Broadway that people come to from far and wide to see the ball drop in Times Square on New Year's Eve or to see the Broadway plays for which New York City is so well known. However, being some five miles north of Times Square and the city's theater district, Hamilton Heights is another take on both Broadway and New York City.

Though I do not remember anything like tumbling into the world ten minutes after my sister or when I started to walk or talk, I do remember being intrigued by the moving sunlight that reflected up and onto our ceiling from the cars that passed on the street below. Cruising with my sister in our carriage, being weaned from the baby bottle, sitting in our playpen, learning to tie my shoes, learning how to cross the street, and dining at our child-sized table are all very clear memories for me too. Knowing how ticklish I am, intentionally and playfully, my mother used to tickle my feet when she put my socks on and would try to convince me that it was by accident. Then when I, reluctantly, put my foot out, she would tickle it again. I also remember the way my father rolled oranges on the tabletop under his hand until they were soft; then with his pocketknife, he would punch a hole in the top of the orange; and from the opening, we would drink the fresh and sweet juice right from the orange. Born and raised in Florida, this was very likely something that his father did for him when he was a kid.

Learning to write the letters of the alphabet is another clear memory of mine. I so much admired my mother's handwriting, and I wanted more than anything to form my letters as nicely as she formed hers. Hardly able to appreciate the charm and beauty that I see in a child's less-than-perfect handwriting now, I had no choice other than to continue frowning at my own chicken scratch until it eventually got better. For as long as I can remember, seeing birds fly was something that easily caught and held my attention. Watching them jump and spread their wings to glide over trees and rooftops might have been my biggest thrill. With much desire and plenty of wishful thinking, I was sure that I would soon sprout a pair of wings of my own someday, and would soon be able to fly, too. Had I been given a choice, I would have traded my arms and hands in for a pair of wings without a second thought. Unlike most small boys' fascination with fire engines, I, instead, was fascinated by garbage trucks. Whenever I heard them pull into the block, I perched myself at one of our living room windows to watch the men toss the garbage into the heavy machinery at the back end of the truck to be chewed up, swallowed down, and carried away.

Another memory of mine was my mother's knack for telling stories. She would put her amazing storytelling gift to use when an occasional power outage caused our lights to go out. So whenever we found ourselves in the dark, we would gather at our kitchen table with a candle and a bowl of pecans in the middle. Then, in no time, we would find ourselves riveted to our seats, and completely engrossed by one of her captivating stories. Oddly enough, as much of a disappointment as it was for me when the lights went out, it was always another disappointment when the spell was broken by the lights coming on again, and abruptly tearing us away from the world of fantasy that my mother had taken us to, off the cuff and right from the top of her head.

Our father, an ex-military man, was not as talkative as my mother. Not inclined to superfluous chatter, he tended to speak mostly when it was necessary. Nevertheless, he was a very good father, and he did an excellent job of taking care of our small family. He seemed to particularly enjoy sitting back to read the newspaper or to take in the world around him through his cloud of cigar smoke, as he watched us scooting around on the floor, or in our playpen in front of him. My father had a real knack for fixing things. So if I came to him with a broken toy or anything else in need of repair, when he finished with it and handed it back to me, without fail, it would function as well or look as good as new, if not better.

The thing that our parents did have in common was the care with which they looked after us. Though they were not the types of parents who smother their children in hugs and kisses, we felt their love in other ways. If my father was not at work, feeding us lunch, or helping us wash our small hands, he would take us to either one of our two neighborhood parks. Time, energy, effort, or expense did not seem to matter when it came to providing us with things to do. Not only that, but he was always willing to bring any of the neighborhood kids along who wanted to join us.

For being the imposing figure he was, I can say there was only one time that he ever resorted to corporal punishment with any of us. Much to his credit, he was advanced in his approach to parenting and generally well ahead of his time in many other ways too. As proud as I am to cite this small bit of my family's history when it did happen, it was you truly who was on the receiving end.

A blowout between my sister and me hit the fan and spun out of control before either of us knew what happened. The next thing I knew was that I felt a slipper bounce off the side of my head; then in a harmless attempt to retaliate, I tried to hit her on the least vulnerable part of her arm, just below her shoulder; but instead, I hit her in the eye, right before it puffed up and swelled shut. A considerable departure from the way disagreements were handled under our parent's roof, I knew right away that a price would be paid for my mistake and poor judgment. When my father heard the tail end of the commotion and saw my sister's eye, he took me by one of my arms, swung me into position, and popped me once on the seat of my pants. To my surprise, his swat didn't hurt; and I could tell that he held back considerably with it. A full blast from one of his hands would have been epic; and though I deserved much more than what I got, in the end, and to my good fortune, my father's swat was more symbolic than punitive.

Had my mother been home, I would have not gotten off so easily, and I'd be telling a completely different story. Scolding me verbally, or sending me to my room was not always her way of doing things; so corporal punishment was not a problem for her at all. When we were smaller, she used to lay us across her lap and give us one of those old-fashioned spankings with her hand. After outgrowing that, the belt entered the picture. Then if any of us dared to get in trouble while visiting our grandparents in South Carolina, instead of using a belt she would get a thin branch from a bush in the backyard, pull the leaves off, and make her point very clearly with it. I was a respectful, considerate, courteous, and thoughtful kid. But there were still those times when I did things that I should have thought through more carefully. So whenever I had a lapse in judgment, the belt or the dreaded "switch" always helped me to see and remember exactly where I had gone wrong.

Once while visiting my grandparents, my grandfather asked me to bring him his newspaper from the front porch. I don't know what I was thinking that day, but in a slightly offhanded way, I asked him why couldn't he get it himself. Though hardly an acceptable way for a child to speak to his grandfather, it seemed like a perfectly reasonable question to me. But he didn't see it that way, and my mother didn't see it that way either after he told her what I said. After hearing about my snarky reply to my grandfather's request, my mother wasted no time finding and pulling the leaves off of one of those thin branches to show her disapproval; and, unlike my father's spanking, my mother's spanking, as I recall, was quite memorable, and quite clearly did I get her message.

There was another time in South Carolina when my curiosity got me in trouble. While my grandfather sat in his rocking chair watering the lawn, I thought if I could get a good running start, I would be able to break through the stream of water and get only a drop or two of water on me. After mulling it over and one or two false starts, I took off like an airplane headed down a runway, right towards the stream of water. When I hit the water (or I should say, when the water hit me) I heard a loud thud, and in an instant, I was drenched from head to toe. Now I had to face my mother, wet clothes and all. It might have helped if I had explained to her why I did it. On the other hand, since I had just changed into the clean and freshly pressed outfit that she had just spruced up for me, it might have not helped at all. Nonetheless, when I saw her walking towards the backyard, I knew that another plant was going to pay the price for me finding out the hard way that I didn't run as fast as I thought, and how ridiculous this idea of mine was.

One other time I found myself in trouble back at home in NYC. At my insistence, my mother bought a Superman suit for me. Happily, I tore the box open and unfolded my new red, yellow, and blue cape, suit, and boots. My happiness was short-lived when I tried the suit on and saw how badly it fitted. It hung from my skinny frame like it would hang from a skeleton, showing not even the slightest bit of my nonexistent muscle tone. So, much to my disappointment, my new Superman suit fitted me nothing like the way Superman's suit fitted him.

Trying to find a solution, I thought if I put a layer of clothing on under the suit, it might help me to fill it out more. But when I looked in the mirror again, my attempted remedy only made me look like a lumpy version of Superman. When that didn't work, I became frustrated again. Then I started to cry and complain about how poorly the suit fitted. As I continued to cry and complain, my mother eventually reached her limit. Her sympathy shifted to tolerance; then she became annoyed, and before I knew it, she'd had enough. As she came at me with one end of a belt wrapped around her hand, I tried to get out of the line of fire by jumping onto my bed and scampering over to the other side. Out of the corner of my eye, I could see my cape flapping behind me as I tried to get away. As funny as it must have been to see a skinny, lumpy, and cowering version of Superman beating a hasty retreat, my mother was not amused at all. Given all of the drama I caused with my crying and complaining, there was no chance of me being let off the hook any easier. She must have gotten four or five swats in before it was over.

Interestingly enough, this was the first and only spanking of hers that didn't hurt. So, as I thought at first, it had nothing to do with me wearing an impenetrable Superman suit; instead, it was the padding from the extra clothing I had on underneath that saved me that time. Clearly, this was long before they added the six-pack abs and bulging biceps to Superman suits that I see kids wearing now. So when it was all over, I was relieved to have gotten away with a pain-free spanking that time, and I never put the suit on again.

So despite having the seat of my pants dusted off every now and then, I had no doubt that my mother loved me in that special way that mothers love, nurture, and protect their sons. Hardly a day goes by without me being reminded of this when I see mothers lovingly and caringly teach, explain, and point out new, fun, and interesting things to their sons about the world around them, something that is not unlike that special bond between fathers and daughters.

When it was time to leave the hospital, my mother and sister were the only ones cleared to go home. I, on the other hand, was not released. Whatever the doctor picked up on, he thought it was enough for them to keep me. I was asthmatic, and I had allergic reactions to just about everything. Additionally, whatever I ate would soon bounce right back up and out of my mouth. Then along with that, I had occasional bouts of nose bleeding that started and stopped for no apparent reason. Though 506 W. 151st Street was my first home address, much of my time was spent as an inpatient at the Columbia Presbyterian Hospital in Washington Heights.

Despite the concerns my health issues caused, it was a blessing in disguise. On a personal note of sorts, when it was time for me to undergo the ritualistic knife that is (supposedly) for male hygienic purposes, cultural traditions, or religious beliefs, the doctor did not sign off on it. As my father explained to me years later, the doctor did not think it would be good to subject me to something so invasive, given my condition. This was a very lucky break for me; another lucky break was that my father explained it all to me when I was older. Not the easiest thing to talk to a 10-year-old about, he could have said nothing and left it all a mystery that I would have never been able to figure out on my own. But by taking the time to talk to me about it, not only did he provide me with a bit of my own personal history, but he provided me with more of a complete picture of who I am and why. Having sidestepped the knife himself too somehow, he had no qualms about the doctor's very wise words and thoughtful decision. Additionally, despite the private and personal nature of all of this, going under a cold knife of any kind is hardly what I would have chosen for myself if I had a say in the matter. Though male children never seem to have any conscious memory of being circumcised, I am not convinced that a trauma of that magnitude does not come with some kind of residual emotional or psychological scaring for males, or females (in other parts of the world) for that matter. Along with that, I don't feel that I missed out on anything particularly special, and I much prefer having all of the body parts I entered the world with, despite the popular opinion to the contrary on the matter. Now, I am always amazed when I hear people speak of circumcision as some kind of special honor, privilege, or favor.

Getting to the bottom of my array of health issues made it necessary for me to spend one of my Christmas holidays in the hospital. During my stay, I did my best to entertain myself by looking at the colorful Christmas lights, watching the large snowflakes fall, and watching people walk around outside from my hospital room window. I remember getting a wooden jigsaw puzzle from Santa Claus when he visited us kids one day, so that kept me busy and entertained for a little while.

Once while sitting on my hospital bed, looking out the window, bored out of my skull, and wanting to go home more than anything, I heard a voice come out over the hospital's public address system. The voice sounded like my mother's voice, and though I could not understand what the garbled voice said, I was sure that it was my mother who had come to take me home. So I jumped off the bed, ran out of my room, and dashed down the hallway, expecting to find her. With her nowhere to be found, a nurse soon had me by the hand, and before I knew it, I was back in my room, on my bed, looking at the people outside, the falling snow, and Washington Heights' colorful Christmas lights again.

With time and good medical care, clear signs of improvement in my health started to appear, and eventually, I outgrew my assortment of childhood illnesses. The Columbia Presbyterian Medical Center did an excellent job of taking care of me. My food started to stay down, the causes of my allergies were pinpointed, and my episodes of nose bleeding stopped. I was then finally released from the hospital. I did have to go to the hospital's clinic for weekly checkups and shots. So, once a week, my mother and I took the bus up to Columbia Presbyterian's clinic. When calling me up to be seen by the doctor, the receptionists could never seem to get my name right: "Uhhhhh, Berol Spigots?" was one of the many versions that I remember hearing. Then my mother and I would just look at each other and laugh. These medical appointments were hardly my favorite pastime, but by that time, I had become so used to all of the hospitals poking and probing that I simply took it all in stride.

During one of these appointments, I experienced something that I never forgot. A very special nurse who saw me that day stood head and shoulders above all of the other nurses I'd seen previously. Unlike the others who impersonally did the once over with a ball of cotton before hitting me with needles like they were throwing darts, this nurse took a completely different approach. From the moment she entered the examining room,

I was taken by how polite, kind, and personable she was, and how she included me in her talk with my mother. She told me that the injection was going to take a little longer than usual this time, but she assured me that it would not hurt. Then she asked me to relax and asked me not to tighten my muscles.

As I assumed the all too familiar position across my mother's lap and braced myself for the needle's sting, I did exactly as she asked; and true to her words, the injection did not hurt at all. The injection took about ten seconds, but I did not feel a thing. I didn't even feel the discomfort or pressure while the medicine was being injected, and then she gave me a bright red lollypop. By that time, I had been completely swept off my feet. Given the very personal touch that this Florence Nightingale of a nurse added to her care, she left one of those good and lasting impressions on me. Along with that, I thought she was pretty and had a nice smile too; so at no more than four years old, I experienced my first crush that day. Then to my misfortune, I never saw her again after that appointment, and it was back to the dart-throwing nurses again.

Christmas was always a special time in our household. There was always plenty of snow during that time of year, so a Christmas mood was set that could have not been better. Since we didn't have a chimney or a fireplace, I thought long and hard about how Santa Claus entered our apartment. I had no idea if he parked his sled on the sidewalk and came up the stairs to our front door, or if he came through our living room window after landing his sled and team of reindeer on our snow-covered fire escape. I never asked my parents about it, but as long as there were gifts under our tree on Christmas Day, how Santa entered our apartment was not my overriding concern.

It did not seem possible for things to get better as we prepared for this special day. I was very much taken by it all, and it was a tossup, for me, between Christmas and birthdays in terms of which one is better. Be it visiting Santa Claus at the department stores, shopping for our tree, or decorating it, it was all just as exciting and fun for me as Christmas Day itself. Christmas Day preliminaries notwithstanding, there were always loads of nicely wrapped gifts for us that included any special requests we made in our letters to Santa Claus.

Two of my most memorable Christmas presents were a Howdy Doody puppet and an electric train set. The puppet had a string attached to the back of its head that made its mouth and chin move up and down, and the train puffed smoke from its smokestack. Of course, there were plenty of cap pistols and holsters. During that time, there was probably no better way for my brother and me to enjoy Christmas than running around and shooting cap pistols at each other. Over the years I was given a chemistry set, roller skates, a tricycle, a bicycle, a movie projector, a microscope, a sled, and even a pool table. One special gift was a six-inch stuffed replica of a sailor that I took a special liking to, and, in no time, it had become my close friend and a part of our family, as far as I was concerned.

On one of those Christmas mornings, I found a pair of boxing gloves and a speed bag under the tree with my name on it. Eager to give it a try, I attached the bag to the flexible metal pole that screwed into a floorboard, slipped my hands into my new boxing gloves, took my stance, and jabbed at the bag one or two times before lowering the boom. Then I reached back and hit the bag as hard as I could, throwing everything I had into the punch. The bag went half the distance to the floor, sprung back, and hit me in the nose. It took several seconds for the birds and stars I saw circling around my head to clear out, but my Christmas Day festivities had to be put on hold until a cold compress was able to bring some relief to my bloody nose. To this day, I am convinced that there were at least two very clear messages for me about ducking and keeping my hands to myself.

Christmas Eve, with all of its trappings, was what I enjoyed most of all. For the small price of staying in my room, I knew that there would be plenty of gifts under our tree the next morning. Though buzzing with excitement, somehow I managed to stay in my room and sleep throughout the night. It was a small price to pay, given all that I would get in return.

As I started to get up there in age, my mother must have thought that it was time to fill me in a little bit more about Santa Claus and Christmas. After her talk, she assured me that it would have no impact on our Christmas gifts. The news of it all was not an easy pill for me to swallow; but with our Christmas gifts still a part of the picture, I was okay with the surprising bit of news that she had for me that day.

Up the street from our building and on the other side of Amsterdam Avenue was (and still is) the Carmansville Playground. The park was named after Richard Carman, a landowner in the area during the early 1800s. He earned a fortune by rebuilding much of the southern end of Manhattan after (what was called) the Great Fire of 1835.

The Carmansville Playground was a half block away, just inside Sugar Hill; it was the perfect place for a quick escape for some fun, recreation, fresh air, and sunshine. It was the first playground I had ever played in, or had ever seen for that matter. In spite of its hard and coarse concrete surface, it was a fun place to spend hot summer days. It had swings, seesaws, sliding boards, sprinklers, and areas set aside for tennis, handball, and basketball. Carmansville was the first place I saw basketball being played, too. Much later, it was popularly known as the "battlegrounds" among some of NYC's best basketball players, including Kareem-Abul Jabbar. As I watched the older kids enthusiastically charge up and down the court, little did I know that I would be doing the same thing years later, or that basketball would become Harlem's, New York City's, and perhaps the nation's most beloved sport. Basketball hoops can be found on urban playgrounds, or in suburban driveways practically everywhere these days. Along with that, basketball arenas are filled to the rafters from coast to coast with enthusiastic fans, and the game is played and loved by people around the world, much like football and baseball.

In the opposite direction and about three blocks from our building is the Ten Mile River Playground. It is between the Henry Hudson Parkway and the Hudson River; it has grass, trees, and a beautiful view of the Hudson River, Palisades Amusement Park (at that time), the George Washington Bridge, and a view of New Jersey's eastern coastline. Our father took us there to play in the sandpits with our small buckets and shovels. I remember the fresh, clean scent of the sand as if it were yesterday. Then when I was older, my father took me there with a baseball bat, a ball, and a pair of baseball gloves. There he taught me how to throw, catch, and hit. As much as he loved baseball, nothing would have pleased him more than me becoming a professional baseball player. He absolutely loved the game, and he spent a lot of time teaching me its fundamentals.

With the Brooklyn Dodgers being the pioneers they'd become, breaking baseball's ironclad color barrier in 1947, it was only natural that the people of Harlem were diehard Dodger and Jackie Robinson fans. In the same way that there were those who shot their stress and blood pressure levels up because Barack Obama became the nation's 44th president, there were those who spent plenty of sleepless nights over Jackie Robinson playing major league baseball. Though all of this happened a year before I was born, Dodger Mania was still alive and well in Harlem when I was old enough to understand and appreciate the game. I was so much of a Dodger fan that I knew the team's batting order and roster as well as the commentators calling the games. I remember these larger-than-life ballplayers, and I can still hear their names being called out at the start of each game and when they came up to bat: Jackie Robinson, Roy Campanella, Pee-Wee Reese, Jim Gilliam, Carl Furillo, Don Drysdale, Johnny Padres, Roger Craig, Duke Snider, Don Zimmer, Sandy Kofax, Don Newcombe, and Gil Hodges. The Dodger's home stadium was Ebbets Field in Brooklyn, and the team's manager was Walter Alston.

Despite Harlem's love for the Dodgers, my father was a steadfast Yankee fan. At the time, the Yankees had such greats as Mickey Mantle, Elston Howard, Yogi Berra, Whitey Ford, Bill Skowron, Enos Slaughter, and Bobby Richardson; and their manager was Casey Stengal. Roger Maris joined the team years later. My mother was both a Dodger and a Giant fan. Before the Giants moved to San Francisco, their home stadium was the Polo Grounds, which was only a few blocks from where we lived. Willie Mays, Joey Amalfitano, Alvin Dark, Dusty Rhodes, and Whitey Lockmon were some of the players who made up the Giants' roster. With New York City having three baseball teams (at that time) and the three (or four) diverging team loyalties under our roof, bragging rights and baseball banter were rife and energetic whenever one of our favorite teams won or lost. Affectionately, the Dodgers were known as the Brooklyn Bums, and the Yankees were called the Bronx Bombers. I do not remember the Giants having a nickname, but they were well known for their star centerfielder,

"The Say Hey Kid," Willie Mays. With his signature and very stylish "breadbasket catch," he thrilled crowds everywhere. He positioned himself so that he was able to make these catches right at his beltline, right before throwing a bullet to home plate to catch a base runner trying to score on a sacrifice fly. There was a billboard poster of Willie Mays near the corner of Amsterdam Avenue and 151st Street. It was an ad for a popular brand of pancakes or pancake syrup, and it was there for as long as I can remember; so to this day, I still think of pancakes whenever I think of Willie Mays, or hear his name mentioned.

In 1955 when the Dodgers beat the Yankees in the final game of the World Series, Brooklyn celebrated enthusiastically; but our small neighborhood in Hamilton Heights celebrated enthusiastically too. At the end of the dramatic final game, the Dodgers came roaring back to win the series after losing the first two games. When they did, 151st Street instantly exploded with celebration. Every window on our block was wide open with people waving banners, tossing confetti, sounding noisemakers, and screaming at the top of their lungs; car horns blared, and everyone was thrilled. It was a spontaneous block party the likes of which I had never seen in our quiet neighborhood.

Even though the Dodgers' home turf was a good 20 miles from our neighborhood, and Yankee Stadium no more than 2 miles away, hands down, Harlem backed the Dodgers all the way. Given the profound social statement made by Jackie Robinson and the Dodgers' general manager, Branch Rickey, this affection for the team was an inevitable fact of life. With the display of character and courage that was the hallmark of Jackie Robinson's spectacular career and the Dodgers' vision and legacy as an organization, I too became very much a part of Dodger mania.

I took a special liking to play first base. I studied the mechanics and details of it all by watching Gil Hodges closely. Given my lanky frame, I had the makings for a good first baseman. So it was not hard for me, at all, to figure out which position suited me best. Baseball had become so important to me that I spent much of my time watching games on television, collecting and flipping baseball cards (a game we played), and chewing the flat pieces of bubblegum that came in each package of cards. Dedicatedly, I worked on my throwing, catching, and hitting. Then, if

I were not playing catch, "running bases," pickup games in our hallway, playing "flies up," or stickball, we would climb the fence to play in the vacant lot across the street. Playing catch, baseball, softball, punchball, stickball, and the like were everything to us. So the vacant lot, across the street, made for a much better place for us to play than our narrow hallway, or on the street in front of our building where cars passed through.

Our small neighborhood had just about everything we needed. A dry cleaning establishment, a grocery store, a candy store, a barbershop, an ice cream parlor, and a very popular barbecue takeout called Sherman's were right up the street on Amsterdam Avenue. What we did not have was a public library. Had there been one, it might have (or might have not) instilled more of a passion in me for books and reading. I would not say that I was a bibliophobe, but I can lay no claim to being a bibliophile during that time either. Now, I realize how much I missed by not being more of an avid reader like so many people I have come to admire over the years. More than anything, I would love to be able to say I was a kid who spent hours by myself with my nose buried in books, but that was not the case. Though I may have spared my eyes years of wear and tear, if I had it to do again, this would indeed be something that I would change.

I hasten to add that this was of my own doing. Reading was very important to my mother, and she told me plenty of times that I should spend more of my time reading. She even took the time to tell me a few things about William Shakespeare, but I was just a little bit too busy with other things to hear about this towering literary figure. My mother was more than diligent about correcting us (or just about anyone she knew well enough) if she heard anything said that went against the rules of a good speech or good grammar. Phrases like, "Where you at?" did not have a chance with her, she swatted them down as soon as she heard them. All it took was those three words to get a sideways glance or a reply that had nothing to do with answering the question. So, regarding books and reading, it was up to me to take her advice and make the best of it. Though she tried, because of baseball and so many other things that easily caught and held my attention, books, and reading did not get as much of my time as I would have liked.

Across the street from the Carmansville playground was Hamilton Heights' police station, and it seemed to add a sense of security to the neighborhood. For the time that we lived there, never once did I see or hear of anything having to do with drug use, muggings, robberies, burglaries, murders, assaults, fistfights, guns, knives, drinking, rowdy public behavior, police harassment, or brutality. For that matter, I never heard of one complaint about the Hamilton Heights Police Department. Though all sorts of red flags go up instantly when African-American people and police are mentioned in the same sentences these days, our honorable and respectful Hamilton Heights police officers were clearly there to do their jobs, nothing more or nothing less. You might be surprised by this remarkable (and little known) piece of Harlem's history; it is not the image that Harlem has had in many cases. Nonetheless, this indeed captures our beautiful Hamilton Heights neighborhood. Given the factors that make crime the problem it is in African-American communities all too often, our cozy and quaint neighborhood should have a place in The Guinness Book of Records for its seemingly zero crime rate.

Along with this zero crime rate and no libraries, there was also a conspicuous absence of bars and liquor stores. This, too, could have had a lot to do with the peace and tranquility we enjoyed. The one and only time I ever saw someone drunk in our neighborhood, I was on my way to school with my sister early one morning. Noteworthy is the fact that the inebriated man was not from our neighborhood, nor was he African-American. As we started our walk up Amsterdam Avenue, I saw seven or eight police officers standing around him while he sat on the ground in front of the police station. Though he was not saying anything, he appeared to be a pretty belligerent fellow given how angrily and contemptuously he glared around at everyone, including me. The police were not mistreating him in any way, and they appeared to be trying to decide how to resolve the matter. There was a long string of slime hanging from his nose and mouth that went all the way to the ground; so the police seemed to be thinking long and hard about how to handle the matter with as little physical contact as possible.

When the man looked at me, it appeared that he was going to say something to me for looking at him, given the scowl on his face when our eyes met; but he didn't say a word. Then, right when it appeared that he was seconds away from unloading a stream of expletives at me, I saw his eyes glaze over and focus elsewhere. It seemed as if he thought better of saying something rude to a six-year-old kid, or my image could have been suddenly washed away by something else occupying his alcohol-soaked state of mind. Though I had no way of knowing where he was from or how he ended up in our neighborhood, the police apparently came up with a solution, because everything was back to normal when we passed the police station on our way home later that afternoon.

Visiting my grandparents in South Carolina was always a nice change from the city life we lived. Soon after school let out on June 30th, my mother, my siblings, and I would head to Pennsylvania Station in Midtown to take the "Silver Meteor" for the long train ride to Columbia, South Carolina. I do not know how long it took to get there, but I passed the time eating, sleeping, or watching the trees, telephone poles, telephone wires, and crisscrossing train tracks as they shot by the windows of our fast-moving train.

After arriving, the first thing I always noticed was the fresh and clean scent of the country air. Since our train always pulled into the station late at night, we were thrilled by seeing the lightning bugs (fireflies) that hung in mid-air, flashing their lights right in front of our eyes. To me, they were magical and were like nature's welcoming committee putting on a light show for us and the other passengers as we stepped down and off the train.

My grandfather enjoyed relaxing in his rocking chair, smoking cigars, and reading the newspaper. While he held his newspaper up, my siblings and I loved to sneak up to bash our hands into the paper while he read. He would then playfully shoo us away by loudly rustling his newspaper at us, and acting as if he were going to get out of his chair to come after us. We would then scatter running and laughing from the fun of it all. Every morning, I would wake up to the smell of grits, bacon, eggs, coffee, and biscuits. Then by the time I made my way to the table, there would be a spread of food that never failed to get my day off to a good start.

Along with the fresh air, lightning bugs, and southern-styled cooking, I loved my grandparents' backyard. It reminded me of the open country where cowboys once roamed. With dirt paths, grass, and trees as far as I could see, it was the perfect place for me to immerse myself in two of my other favorite pastimes of being a cowboy and eating jelly and peanut butter sandwiches. So if I were not riding around on a broom handle with a belt fastened to it, straddling a chair backwards worked just as well for being my galloping horse.

There was a large pecan tree in the backyard that left tasty pecans all over the ground. My grandmother grew collard greens in her garden, and there were dark tasty grapes that grew on a vine around her backyard. The backyard provided us with all kinds of fun things to do that were not possible to do in NYC. My brother and I climbed trees, threw rocks, ate jelly and peanut butter sandwiches outside, and tied sheets and blankets to trees to make tents. These makeshift tents provided us with a small amount of relief from the blazing hot southern summer sun.

A kid named Horace Mack was the first person I remember meeting who spoke with a Southern accent. I imagine that we must have sounded just as strange to him, but he did not seem to be much troubled by our New York accents. He was, however, surprised to learn that my sister and I did not know what "grub" means. One day he told us that he was going to go home to get some grub. Hearing this, my sister and I looked at each other with puzzled facial expressions. Then perfectly timed, we both asked him about this new and strange-sounding word, "What's grub?" Just as startled by our question, and with every bit of his accent behind his reply, he asked: "What's grub?" "You mean to tell me y'all don't know what grub is?" His question as well as his delivery echoed in our heads for the longest time and remained a source of childhood mirth and wonderment, for us, for years to come.

Horace Mack never wore shoes, and he was able to walk over broken glass, jagged rocks, and pebbles with ease. Much taken by this, there was no way that I was not going to give it a try. After slipping out of my shoes and socks, it didn't take long for me to realize that he made it look a lot easier than it actually is. As I attempted to follow along in his footsteps, the pain at the soles of my feet was unbearable as I grimaced and gingerly stepped on small rocks and all kinds of other pointed, hard, and painful objects.

Not wanting to give up without giving it a good try, I hobbled along behind him until I learned what it really means to walk around, outside, in South Carolina without shoes. This time it involved a shoeless trip to the corner store one day. As I walked across the surface of my grandparent's cool and freshly watered lawn, I had no idea of what awaited me before I jumped down onto the blazing hot concrete sidewalk. As soon as my feet hit the hot surface, I felt the heat penetrate the soles of my feet, and it seemed to ring a loud bell at the pain center receptors of my brain. Instead of going back to get my shoes, the only thing I could think to do was to take off running in the direction of the store, hot feet and all; and it felt as if the bottom of my feet were on fire.

Once inside the store, the cool sawdust on the floor soothed my feet as the screen door slammed shut behind me. Momentarily distracted by all of the things to buy, the reality of the half-block trip back was something that I had not yet fully considered. When it was time to leave, I took several seconds to prepare myself and took off running. With my feet not yet recovered from the initial trip, the return trip was worse, and it seemed to take twice as long. While I ran, it felt as if I were running across the surface of a large and hot frying pan, and I promised myself to never come outside without shoes on ever again. With my feet heating up more and more with each step, I finally made it to the wall that separated the sidewalk and my grandparents' elevated lawn. I jumped up and onto the lawn's cool and moist surface, and it felt as if my feet had sizzled in relief, and this was when and where my shoeless adventure in South Carolina came to an end.

Another lesson for me about the searing heat of the southern sun came on another very hot day. This time, from my grandparent's living room window, I saw a woman walking by with an umbrella up. Though quite normal and customary in the South, I had never seen anyone in NYC with an umbrella up when it wasn't raining. When I called my mother to see what I thought was the oddest thing ever, I must have made a pretty big fuss about it, because when she came to see what had me so worked up, she assured me that it was nothing to be so startled about. Then she explained that it was common for women to use umbrellas in the South to protect themselves from the sun. Then in an instant, the strangest thing I thought I'd ever seen made sense to me, and my mother had solved another one of my many childhood mysteries.

Going to church with my grandmother was indeed one of my bigger challenges. Unlike the hour we spent in church in NYC, whenever we went to church with her, I had to plan on being there for much longer than one hour. Very often, we spent the entire day there. During these daylong church services, the fun-filled activities that I looked so much forward to vanished with each tick of the clock.

The preacher was like a freight train once he locked himself into his stride. Bolstered and egged on by the congregation, a sermon could go on, seemingly, forever. Doing my best to weather the storm, I would end up dazed, hungry, frustrated, restless, hot, and numb from sitting in one place for so long. There was one time when my mother and grandmother couldn't help but laugh when I leaned over, slightly annoyed, and asked what was he so angry about, and why did he have to shout so much.

Another one of our great summer getaways took us to Hampton, Virginia during the summer of 1956. My sister, Doris, and her husband were close to welcoming their first and only child into the world. So to lend a helping hand (with our luggage and the three of us in tow) my mother was on her way to Pennsylvania Station again. As in South Carolina, what was most striking to me was the scent of the fresh country air.

My sister's husband was a Master Sergeant in the U.S. Army and they lived in a beautiful split-level home near the army base. I was amazed at the size and beauty of the house as Doris gave us a guided tour soon after we arrived. There was a screen-enclosed front porch that kept the mosquitoes away while we talked, played checkers, watched the lightening bugs, listened to the crickets, and breathed in the fresh, sweet country air.

Across the roadway and right in front of the house was a large moat that surrounded an old army fort. I used to go to the moat in the morning with a string tied to a crabbing basket to catch the large crabs that came quickly to feed on practically anything I used for bait, and then I would let them go. In the evening, when my sister's husband came home, we washed up and gathered at the dining room table for one of Doris' tasty meals. While we ate, Ricky filled us in on whatever happened at the army base during the day. If anyone were the embodiment of an ad for joining the army, it was my brother-in-law. From his shiny brass belt buckle, spit-shined boots, and his perfectly pressed uniform, it was clear how seriously he took his service to the army and his rank of Master Sergeant.

During our stay, my nephew, Duane, was born. It was nice to be there to welcome him into the world. Though it seemed odd being an uncle at only eight years old, I was an uncle nonetheless, and my siblings and I were crazy about him as soon as we saw him.

When our trips south ended, we boarded the huge train again for the ride back up to NYC. After leaving the train station for the cab ride home, there was always another round of culture shock that I felt as much as the one I felt when we arrived in the South. Being the very distinct regions that the two places are, it was always exciting for me to return to NYC. Be it the tall buildings, the crowds of people, the way the heat and humidity hung in the air, or the way the car horns echoed against the tall buildings, it felt as if I were arriving to NYC for the first time. Then just as well, it was ever so clear to me that I was home once again.

The Harris family lived down the hall from us; and their daughter, Carol never let anyone forget that her full name was "Carol Ann Harris." Her mother and father were my parent's closest friends. Carl Patterson, another one of our playmates from the building, would often tell us that he couldn't play with us for too long because he had to go to work soon. As outlandish as his cooked-up story sounded to me, I was amazed at the lengths he took to convince us that he was a part of the adult workforce, at no more than five or six years old. Mr. and Mrs. Robinson managed the building and they lived in an apartment in the basement with their three daughters Pricilla, Margie, and Bunky (aka. Geraldine "Bunky" Robinson as she clearly made it known). Another one of our childhood playmates, Diane Collins, had a Doberman pinscher named Prince, and very proudly she let us know that she chose the dog's name. Apparently, names were very important for many of our childhood neighbors and friends. A woman named Mrs. Eulick lived right below us, and whenever our horseplay became too much for her, she responded by thumping her broom handle against her ceiling.

Then there was a woman who lived on the third floor whose name I never knew, nor do I remember ever seeing her. But, she had a ferocious dog that barked and snarled at anyone who walked by her door, and it terrorized me for most of the time we lived there. Had there been another way for me to get home, I would have taken it because my heart would be in my throat whenever I walked by her door. The dog barked, growled, and snarled into the space under the door in a way that sent chills up my spine. By the way that it rattled and slammed into the door, it sounded as if it were three times my size, and seconds away from breaking the door down to get me. Making matters worse, the woman never scolded the dog or did anything to quiet it down. So for my own peace of mind, I figured out that if I stepped ever so lightly, I could get by the door without riling up this aggressive dog. I could hear my heart beating as I walked by listening to the dog breathe, sniff, and snort at the small space under the door as if to let me know that he knew I was there. Another fear of mine was the roar of motorcycles. While out and about, my parents knew, all too well, that if I heard a motorcycle before they did when they looked down, all they would see was the space I was standing in, and maybe the last bit of dust settling that I kicked up when I took off running. With a little bit of help, I was able to overcome this fear of mine pretty quickly. When I started to see the ice cream vendors, on Riverside Drive, who sold their ice cream on motorcycles with built-in freezers attached to the sides, it did not take long before the sound of motorcycles meant a whole new thing to me.

Along with my mother's knack for telling stories, she was a very good piano player too, and playing for people may have been her biggest thrill. For as long as I can remember, there was always a piano in our living room, and pianos have been somewhat of a tradition in our family. My grandmother, my mother, and both of my sisters have had pianos and have all played to varying degrees. I have an electric keyboard in my living room now, and though I cannot say that I am a piano player, I do know piano fundamentals, I know how to read piano music, and I would very likely be a halfway decent hack of a piano player if I had continued practicing as much as I did at one time. I can teach piano basics and piano theory; then too, plenty of times, I used to see my brother seated at the piano figuring out a tune or two.

When we moved from Hamilton Heights, one of the household items that did not make the trip was our old and beautiful upright piano. But before we were completely settled into our new apartment, a brand new Spinet was wheeled into our living room. Never once during that time did I think having a piano, or having a parent who played music would factor into my life in any way. But each one did and did so rather significantly. Whatever it was about my mother that gave her such an appreciation for music, she passed it on to us in the same way it was passed to her by her mother previously. My mother never played professionally, but given how much she enjoyed playing, it took no coaxing at all to get her to run her fingers over the keys for a song or two. Her favorite songs were "Sentimental Journey" and "Mood Indigo," and she was always quick to give free lessons to any of our friends who showed the slightest interest in learning.

My father, on the other hand, seemed to have not even the slightest interest in music. Given the roles that blues, jazz, and gospel have played in African-American life, I now find (what appeared to be) his indifference to music quite interesting. Not once did I ever see him lift the lid to look at one of its eighty-eight black and white keys, nor did I ever hear him utter a word about this large instrument that was always a part of our living room décor. Then too, instead of listening to music, whenever his small transistor radio was on, it was always tuned to a Yankee game.

With one of my many silly child-like (why is the sky blue-type) questions, I asked my father if music is good for you. I don't know what prompted me to ask him such an off-the-wall question, but given his affirmative reply, I at least know now that he did not think music is a complete waste of time. I do know for a fact that he was not all that taken by football. He told me as much, once when he expressed how senseless he thought it is for football players to work so hard to improve their strength and conditioning, to soon break each other up by crashing, colliding, and piling on top of each other. Seeing my brother and me imitating what we saw football players doing, with socks padding the shoulders of our T-shirts, and football more and more catching our attention, I think that it was his attempt to steer us clear of anything having to do with football. Taking the concussions and all of the other debilitating football-related injuries into consideration, I have to say again that my father was insightful, ahead of his time, and on to something that no one really talked about, until only recently. Then when it came to basketball, I never heard him say a word about it. My guess is that he may have been as lukewarm about basketball as he was about music and football. Hands down, baseball was what he liked. With that said, my sister told me only recently that our father was a very big Sarah Vaughn fan; and though my father and I had never as much as once mentioned Sarah Vaughn's name to each other, from as young as 10 years old, I was a big Sarah Vaughn fan too; so as the adage states quite clearly, "The apple does not fall too far from the tree."

Though it was my mother's penchant for music that later shaped a large part of who I am now, I was happy to sit at the piano with the lid closed while watching Liberace play on television as I pretended to play along with him, with my sister doing the same at my side.

Our elementary school, P.S. 46, was six blocks away. The building took up the entire block, so there were more than enough classrooms and space to carry the load. The boys wore shirts and neckties, and the girls wore dresses and skirts. I do not know how the girls did it during the long and brutally cold winter months. Unlike any other school I attended, instead of lining up to walk double file down to an auditorium for assembly, P.S. 46 had its own unique approach to this. The walls dividing our classrooms were on wheels that rolled on a set of tracks. So right before assembly, the walls would be retracted in a way that made it seem as if we had been transported to another location, reseated with our other schoolmates, and facing a podium without leaving our seats. It was an orderly system that was much easier than trying to herd a flock of energetic children down to an auditorium and reseated.

My sister and I made the journey up Amsterdam Avenue to P.S. 46 five days a week. There was a time when I could name all of my teachers right through to the twelfth grade. Now, I have forgotten a name or two, but I do remember the names of all of the others.

I could not wait until I was old enough to go to school. Thrilled by the idea, I beleaguered my mother incessantly with questions about what going to school would be like. But it never occurred to me once that she would not be spending the day there with us. On the first day, we arrived soon after class had started. Everyone was already seated, and my sister and I stood at the front of the classroom while my mother spoke with the teacher briefly. When I saw my mother turn to leave, I take no pride in saying that I lost it, completely. Though my sister had no problem with her leaving, I cried shamelessly right in front of everyone. Then to make matters worse, having no siblings to ease the transition into their first day, my classmates still handled it better than I did. So it was yours truly who stood in front of my new classmates with my mouth stretched wide open while blubbering with tears streaming down the sides of my face. After my mother quietly slipped out the door (without me noticing) no one paid the slightest bit of attention to me in the midst of my dramatic display. My sister appeared to be having a ball given all of the new faces and the possibility of making acquaintances with so many new classmates. Despite the spectacle I made of myself, I soon realized that it was time for me to pull my act together. Then, before long, I was right in there with the rest of the kids and this new routine as if nothing had ever happened. Then on the second day, I could have not been more unperturbed when I saw my mother turn to leave, hoping that everyone had forgotten about my embarrassing first day at school.

P.S. 46 had an all African-American student body. We had the usual curriculum of math, reading, writing, and penmanship. Before school started, in the morning, and after lunch, we played in the schoolyard until the bell rang. Then we formed double lines by sizing each other up with our hands at our foreheads as if we were saluting each other. By doing this, the shorter kids knew to go to the front of the lines, and the taller kids knew to go to the back. We had to stand as straight as an army drill team without anyone slouching or leaning out of line before walking double-file up the staircase to our classrooms.

Each class had a line monitor who wore a badge and a white plastic sash-like belt that went around the waist, across the chest, and over the shoulder. The monitor's job was to be sure that everyone stood perfectly in line, and was not chewing gum, talking, or trying to sneak to get a drink of water after the bell rang. Once a day we were given a break from our schoolwork. During these breaks, we were allowed to put our books, pencils, and papers away, and were given cream-filled wafers and small containers of cold milk. After that, we were allowed to lay our heads on our desks and rest for a half-hour before starting with our work again.

We had a maintenance man who regularly barged into our classroom to clean our windows. While the class was in session, unannounced, he would enter with all of his cleaning supplies rattling and clattering loudly from his utility belt. I remember that his name was Chester, and he always had an unfiltered cigarette hanging from the side of his mouth. It appeared that Chester took great pride in cleaning our windows with his exaggerated and overblown entrance. I watched him as he raised the windows to climb out and onto the windowsill, and fasten his safety belt into hooks at each side of the window. Once fastened in, he would lean back against the support of his safety belt to clean the windows while dangling three or four floors above the concrete surface below as if the possibility of falling did not matter to him at all. Watching him, I became so concerned about him falling that it distracted me enough that it was hard for me to stay focused on the lesson while he was there. To me, it seemed like such a risky way to clean a window. If he had taken a fall one of those times, I would have never been able to get the image out of my head. It was already enough that my vivid and reoccurring dream of him falling interrupted plenty of my otherwise restful nights of sleep. Fortunately, he never fell, and this fear of mine never came to pass.

Occasionally, my parents hosted all-night card parties for their friends. Though these card parties hit their peak long after my siblings and I were fast asleep, breaking up our routine, in this way, was always fun for me. My mother and father cooked large pots of food, prepared snacks, and appetizers for their guests. My siblings and I would then top off our plates and enjoy our small feast before going to bed. Our parents used to store furniture and other household items in our bedroom to create the space needed in the rest of the apartment. After eating, I would eventually pass out from exhaustion after climbing on our bunk bed and over the hodgepodge of household items piled high in our room.

The contrast between the four seasons was something else that I liked. During the year, we experienced the fall, winter, spring, and summer seasons, as well as the distinct ambiance that each one brought to the city. In all of their extremes, we got a taste of the colorful leaves of autumn, the fluffy snow and the blistering cold of winter, the freshness of spring, and the heat, humidity, and green of summer.

Though the winters were extremely cold, the snow was more than we could have asked for as kids. Few things were more exciting than waking up to find the street, rooftops, and cars covered with snow. Then if we were lucky, enough snow would have fallen to close school for the day. On these "snow days" the routine would be broken, and we would put our books away, slip into extra layers of clothing to go out to play in the snow. In spite of the cold, we probably would have played in the snow until we were frozen stiff. Our toes, ears, and fingers would be numb by the time we went upstairs. We climbed the high snowdrifts, rode sleds, built snowmen, or had snowball fights on the same sidewalk in front of our building where we would skate or play stickball under the blazing hot sun in short-sleeved shirts six months later. When we were called upstairs to thaw out and put on a dry change of clothes, our mother would put our wet gloves and socks on the radiator to dry, and she would always have hot buttered toast and a pot of tasty hot chocolate ready, to help warm us up.

On one of these glorious snow days, I rushed downstairs eager to join in on the hot and heavy snowball fight that was already underway. No sooner than I placed one foot out the door, an oversized, stray, and hard snowball smashed into the middle of my face. Then in an instant, my fun-filled snow day was ruined since my swollen lip and bloody nose changed my plans completely.

During the summer months, another popular pastime in our neighborhood was opening the fire hydrant while the kids ran around and played in the water. Because my siblings and I were so young (and perhaps our parents), we never took part in this particular neighborhood activity. So the best we could do was watch it from the front of our building or from our living room window. As you may have seen, kids in NYC are known for opening fire hydrants and directing the flow of water with a tin can opened up at both ends. By placing the can against the opening to the hydrant, they were able to project the water in all directions. They were even able to shoot water high into the air to form an arc of water over the roadway that cascaded down and onto the kids joyfully dancing around on the other side of the street.

With no water shortages to be concerned about, none of the adults seemed bothered by it. Even with the police station being right around the corner, not once did the police come to chase the kids away to turn the water off. So fortunately for the kids, opening the hydrant and playing in the water was a source of fun that was not a problem for anyone, except for the occasional drivers, passing through, who were not able to get their car windows closed quickly enough.

At some point, our first television set was delivered. With its arrival, everything changed. I was able to watch baseball games and many of the television programs that were popular at that time. Amos 'n' Andy, Andy's Gang, Laurel & Hardy, Abbot & Costello, The Little Rascals, Topper,

I Love Lucy, Mighty Mouse, Jackie Gleason and the Honeymooners, Lassie, Heckle and Jeckle, Superman, The Untouchables, Flip the Frog, The Mickey Mouse Club, The Lone Ranger, Roy Rogers, Hop-Along Cassidy, Flash Gordon, The Merry Mailman, Alfred Hitchcock, and Walt Disney were all favorites of mine. On weekends we stayed up late, ate ice cream, snuggled under our blankets, and watched the old black and white classics that the Million Dollar Movie or The Late-Late Show presented each week.

Unlike so much of the unbearable programming, recycled (ghastly, depressing, and useless) news, mayhem, and commercial ads that we pay so much for now, with no more than five or six channels, a flick of the wrist (sometimes with a pair of pliers), and a black and white television set, television was a true source of entertainment for me. Today with state of the art color, high definition, countless channels, 3-D, 72-inch flat screens, remote controls, TiVo technology, DVRs, and the outstanding talent that actors and actresses bring to television these days, television programming (with several very clear exceptions) does not do for me now what it did for me before.

Having the Macy's Thanksgiving Day parade no more than a half hour away was another feature that came with living in Hamilton Heights. We took the subway train down to Central Park West or to Herald's Square where Macy's flagship store is located. As the train pulled into the station, the excitement would build as throngs emptied out, up, and onto the street. We were able to see blowup figures of our favorite cartoon characters and many of television's personalities riding on the parade floats. The music played by the marching bands was exciting and sent chills through me as I listened and watched them play. Experiencing music at that magnitude was a thrill for me, and was the perfect way to get Thanksgiving off to a good start.

This is much of what I remember about my earliest and very fond years of being introduced to the world through the lens of a section of Harlem and Manhattan called Hamilton Heights. I enjoyed our neighborhood, apartment, school, neighbors, and friends very much. But a month or two before turning nine years old, my life in Hamilton Heights ended abruptly. Making matters worse was the fact that I had no forewarning, or the slightest hint that something so major was in the works. I'd come to know and love this neighborhood so much that the move was not easy for me, at all. Then even more significant than that, I had no idea how much this move would change my life.

2

Morningside Heights, Amsterdam Ave. & 125th St.

Our move from Hamilton Heights was probably more traumatic for me than I had ever realized. I have no memory of seeing the old neighborhood for the last time. I don't even remember the twenty-six-block trip to Morningside Heights or how we got there. This perhaps 20 minute timespan is a complete and mysterious blur to me. It were as if a fast-forward button had been pushed, released, and left me sitting on one of our moving boxes in a brand new kitchen, overwhelmed with sadness, and trying to figure out what had happened.

I suspect that two things are responsible for my memory gap. One was certainly the trauma of the move, itself. The other was the fact that my parents, undoubtedly, made a conscious decision to say nothing to me about it beforehand. Knowing them and knowing me, they likely knew the problem that it would have caused. I know how badly I would have reacted to the news, and I am sure they knew it even better than me. So, very cleverly, they devised an airtight plan and executed it with the precision of a Secret Service operation. As a result, I had no idea that something so major was in the works. Then by the time I realized what had happened, everything had been moved, and complaining about it would have been a frustrating waste of time. So there I was with my chin in my hand, feeling sad, helpless, hopeless, and at a loss as to what I could do about it.

Our old apartment building was built at or before the turn of the 20th century, and our new apartment building had just been built. We were the first family to move into apartment 14-I. The building and the apartments were clean, freshly painted, and filling up quickly.

My brother was six years old, and my sister and I were a month or two short of turning nine. I understand, now, that we had no choice other than moving to a larger apartment. With the additional bedroom, my sister had a room of her own. As difficult as the move was for me, having three bedrooms and a modern apartment building did give me some hope. Nonetheless, it still fell short of making up for the fact that our old apartment and neighborhood were things of the past.

Eventually, the new neighborhood started to grow on me. After climbing five flights of stairs for so long, we now had two fast moving elevators that quickly shot us up to the fourteenth floor; this was something new and different for me. Unlike our old building that was five stories high with four apartments on each floor, our new building was twenty-one stories high, and it had eleven apartments on each floor. Then as well, the 1,940 apartment doors of the Ulysses S. Grant Housing Projects had brass doorknockers and peepholes; so these things were new and fancy for me too. So the move felt like an upgrade to me, both economically and socially. Additionally, given the hostile dog in our old building, I was relieved to know that I would no longer have my nerves rattled by any hostile dogs since large pets were not allowed in our new housing units.

On the other side of Amsterdam Avenue were the other five buildings of our nine-building complex. They had been built a year earlier and were full when we moved in. Now, all that remained to be filled were the four buildings on our side of Amsterdam Avenue. With this increase in population density, the opportunity to meet friends had increased exponentially.

Still, somewhat, in shock on that first warm summer night, I laid back quietly on my bed. Our windows were wide open, the smell of fresh paint still hung in the air, and everyone else was already fast asleep. I stared at the reflection of the alternating red and green lights against our ceiling from "Frank's" liquor store fourteen floors below, listened to the chatter of people standing around outside, and listened to the cars that passed through the busy Amsterdam Avenue and 125th Street intersection. At that point, I was resigned to the fact that Hamilton Heights was a bygone era for me.

The next day my sister and I ventured downstairs to see our new neighborhood. One of the first things I saw were several signs posted that listed the playground rules. They were written out clearly on metal signs: "No Bicycle Riding," "No Roller Skating," "No Ball Playing," and "Keep Off Of The Grass." Though troubling at first, most of these rules crumbled under the weight of literally thousands of energetic children and our instincts to run and play.

Discovering the sensory trademarks of our new neighborhood did not take long for me at all. Unlike the smell of steam from the dry cleaners that mixed in with the barbecue sauce from Sherman's BBQ Place in Hamilton Heights, the sound of lawnmowers filled my ears, and the smell of freshly cut grass filled my nose. Then too, there was the smell of some type of chemical spray that was used on the neighborhood's caterpillars. Grant's caterpillars must have been some pretty tough critters; despite the spraying, caterpillars were everywhere. While in the front yard I would regularly feel a tickle or an itch on my arm, neck, or leg. Then when I looked to see what it was, I'd see a confused caterpillar trying to find its way back to its tree. If this proliferation of caterpillars had resulted in half as many butterflies, it would have made for one spectacular sight to see. But the butterfly population never even came close.

To this day, I do not know which rule I broke with the other kids who had gathered to play in the front yard on that second day. Nevertheless, one of the housing guards came up to us slinging his nightstick right before he pulled a thick citation pad from his back pocket. Then, one by one, he asked us for our names and addresses. It was a good thing my sister was there, because I didn't know what our new address was. So when he got to me, I pointed to my sister and told him that my address was the same as hers.

In short order, the kids found names for the housing guards and police officers who patrolled the grounds. The last name of this particular guard was Cortland, so that was what we called him. The guards wore light blue shirts and dark blue pants; and they carried nightsticks, handcuffs, and citation pads. On the other hand, the housing police carried firearms, and they wore the same dark blue uniforms that were worn by New York City police officers during that time.

Of all the Grant Housing police officers, a guy we called "Alley Oop" was most well known. His last name was Grier, but we called him Alley Oop because he was bowlegged, pigeon toed, and he walked like a caveman. The name came from a popular song out at that time about a caveman named Alley Oop. Unlike Cortland, who was a no nonsense guy, Alley Oop had an extra tinge of quirkiness to go along with his generally odd personality, and he didn't seem to be, at all, enchanted by us kids. So the "them and us" lines were quickly drawn in the sand. Whenever the kids saw Alley Oop waddling through the neighborhood, twirling his nightstick, they would start to sing the song: "Alley Oop-boop-boop-boop/boop, Alley Oop-boop-boop-boop/boop. There's a man in the funny papers we all know, Alley-Oop-boop…" Oddly enough, his caveman gait fell right in time with the beat and words to the song. Clearly, it was a risky proposition trying to poke fun at this high-strung, firearm-toting police officer who took his job a bit more seriously than he needed to. Nevertheless, that was what the bold kids from my building did.

Alley Oop soon realized that it was not coincidental that the kids sang the same song whenever he walked by, so he started to turn around to see exactly who the wise guys were in the group. Then as soon as he looked, the singing would stop. Slightly annoyed and unsure of what to do about it, he would continue on his way slinging his nightstick, and shaking his head at the kids' lack of respect for authority.

A few days after being written up by Cortland, notices arrived in our mailboxes indicating our infractions and what our parents needed to pay. He never told us kids what rule we broke, and since we had deliberately done nothing wrong, he could have at least told us what our citations were for, or perhaps let us off with a warning. So these citations were perhaps warnings to let us know how serious they were about enforcing the rules and regulations. Or it could have been a way to generate a little extra cash for Grant's Housing Authority.

Demographic was something else that I liked about our new neighborhood. Unlike Hamilton Heights, that was all African-American, our new housing complex had (and still has) a large Puerto Rican population. My guess is that there was a 50/50 mix between African-American and Puerto Rican families. I liked the way we were mixed in together; it was something pretty special, and it appeared that everyone else liked it too. Very easily the housing authority could have separated us by putting us in different buildings or on different floors given the mood in the country, and the climate it created for segregating people. However, fortunately, nothing like that was ever done. Instead we lived together in all of the nine buildings and on all of the twenty-one floors.

This gave me an opportunity to get to know the Puerto Rican people, and to hear Spanish being spoken for the first time. Both the Puerto Rican people and the Spanish language were hits with me right from the start. I didn't know a word of Spanish, so this was a good thing for me to experience at such an early age. It was both a treat and an education for me to listen to the timbre of this new, exotic, interesting, and expressive language. Along with that, I enjoyed discovering the very different ways that I had to shape my mouth and tongue to articulate the very different types of words. I liked Spanish so much that I promised myself to learn to speak Spanish too, somehow.

Our Puerto Rican neighbors were absolutely great and a lot of fun. Additionally, they clearly had no weird head-trips regarding our cultural differences, and the feeling was mutual. We were a pretty unique community of people, and we learned so much from each other. This was a real eye opener for me, because, until that time, I thought that the entire world had an axe to grind with African-American people. With school desegregation and civil rights struggles at a fevered pitch, I thought that these less than cordial sentiments were universal and simple facts of life. After repeatedly seeing dogs, police, and fire hoses turned on African-American people, it was nice for me to learn that issues regarding race and cultural differences were completely different stories with our new neighbors from Puerto Rico.

The first person I met on the playground that day was a Puerto Rican kid named Louie Diaz. Louie lived right above us in apartment 15-I with his younger brother and sister, Papo and Mary. Their family composition was much like ours. Louie's father was a very funny man named Joe, and everyone affectionately called his wife "Chickie."

Living in the apartment right below the Diaz family, we were regularly treated to Joe's singing since he warmed up his vocal chords, first thing, every morning. The Italian classic "Volare" had to be Joe's favorite song. Like clockwork he would wind up and let it fly enthusiastically, uninhibitedly, in tune, and with impeccable phrasing. "Vooooolare ooh-oh, cantare oh-oh-oh-oh." I didn't know it at the time, but the words mean: "I will fly ooh-oh, I will sing oh-oh-oh-oh." So the song captured Joe's irrepressible joie de vivre persona in every way. More than just singing, I think it was Joe's way of greeting his family, the neighbors, and the world. He was letting us know that he was up, alive, and doing very well. Over the years Joe proved himself to be a true friend and a great neighbor to everyone, as he made every effort to get every ounce of joy he could out of life. Joe was truly one of a kind, and he was able to break my, usually stoic, father up with laughter almost effortlessly.

Louie and I realized that we could talk to each other at the corners of our bedrooms after removing the asbestos padding (between Louie's floor and our ceiling) that surrounded our heating pipes. It was like our own free and secret telephone line. So with nothing more than a tap or two on the pipes (and from the top of my bunk bed), we cracked jokes and laughed until we signed off to go to sleep. This beautiful cultural exchange that emerged from my friendship with Louie was something new for me, and by no means was it an isolated incident. It took place on a much larger scale throughout the entire neighborhood as friendships formed and developed over the years.

I met another kid named Joseph Canales. Joseph and his family lived on the top floor in apartment 21-I. His apartment was positioned in the same rear right-hand corner of the building as Louie's and mine. So whenever I visited Joseph, I was able to see the greatly enhanced view of 125th Street, Harlem, and Manhattan's southeastern skyline from the top floor and from the same rear corner of the building as ours.

Joseph taught me the first Spanish word I learned. While with him one day, it occurred to me that the time was just as good as any to get my Spanish speaking and comprehension underway. So I asked him what the Spanish word is for book; and he told me, "libro." In keeping with the promise I made to myself, I didn't want to forget it. So with a long stretch of my imagination, I made the connection between the words libro and leaf, phonetically. Then after connecting the flat dimensions of a book's pages and that of a leaf, I had my very first Spanish word locked and stored safely in my head. Next Joseph taught me how to count from one to ten. I had no memory trick for that, but out of sheer desire, it was not hard for me to remember at all. At that time, I thought that all I would need to do was learn as many Spanish words as possible, and then substitute them for the English words to be able to speak Spanish. But as I learned, it was not going to be that easy.

Despite the challenges learning a new language involves, it was the start of a long, enjoyable, and rewarding linguistic journey for me that continues to unfold and fascinate me to this day. I imagine that it is much like the thrill a child experiences when he or she learns to speak. Each new word or phrase is like gold, and it is so much fun to put them to use the first few times. Then if you can impress or surprise someone with them, it is even that much more fun. Additionally, being able to speak someone's language, and knowing about them (culturally) are very profound displays of respect. Not only that, but it opens the world up in a very nice and interesting way. This is especially so with the exceptionally friendly Spanish-speaking people from around the world. Regardless of country, skin color, age, male, or female, something that Spanish-speaking people seem to share, other than language, is a genuine sense of warmth, humility, and congeniality. Clearly, this is a deeply ingrained and integral part of the Spanish-speaking culture. Be they from Puerto Rico, Spain, Cuba, Mexico, Panama, Colombia, Peru, Venezuela, or Chile, they are always appreciative of anyone who makes an effort to speak or learn Spanish, and they are more than willing to help by answering any questions about it. Like the Spanish language, they are very beautiful people, and are more than patient, understanding, helpful, and even forgiving about the way people sometimes warp and mangle their beautiful language. Now, I speak Spanish very well, and I still enjoy the process of asking questions, learning, and trying to improve at every opportunity.

Now, when Spanish-speaking people hear me speak, they are surprised to hear that I speak as well as I do. Very often, they tell me that I speak beautifully, and that they hear no trace of an English accent when I speak; some people tell me that I speak with a Puerto Rican accent and others tell me, more often now, that I speak with a Cuban accent. Sometimes, people ask me if either of my parents are Latin American. I love this question, because it gives me a chance to spring one of my favorite jokes on them. Whenever I am asked this question, I start out by telling them that neither of my parents are Latin American. Then I tell them that my mother was born in Colombia. After hearing this, they would usually stop, look at me with a confused expression, and ask me how is it possible for my mother to be from Colombia and not be Latin American. Then I tell them that she is from Columbia, South Carolina. It always gets a good laugh, so I enjoy throwing this hanging curveball whenever someone gives me a chance to.

Joseph's father worked at a bakery, and because of my friendship with Joseph, as a very kind gesture to my family and me, he would bring us bread, cupcakes, rolls, and doughnuts. So before going home, after work, he would come to our house, talk with my parents, and drop off the baked goods. We were very appreciative of his kindness and generosity. As I continued to meet more Puerto Rican people and experience these kinds of things, I was very much gratified by the way they made every effort to reach out to connect with us, the African-American residents at Grant.

Time after time, I'd be invited to a new friend's house to meet their family, and would always be offered food or something to drink. Though I wanted to accept the new, tempting, and tasty food, I would politely decline by saying, "No thank you," as my mother told us to do when we were guests at someone's house. For us, eating at someone's house was lacking in good manners and like asking someone about their income, or answering their telephone. Given the customs and cultural differences between the United States and Puerto Rico, I could tell that my hosts did not quite understand why I would not accept their kind and generous offerings; and I, on the other hand, thought I was doing something good and being respectful by not eating up their food.

With civil rights struggles played out on the news night after night, and so many people buying into the harebrained notion that their lives will be enriched and broadened by confining their circle of friends to people of their own race, national origin, skin color, religion, or cultural background, not once did a single reporter ever come to our neighborhood to report on this highly evolved and sophisticated cultural exchange taking place in our neighborhood and right under their noses. In reality, this was a citywide phenomenon and one of the best things for me to experience while growing up. It would have been a real education for others to see the valuable lessons we learned in our new neighborhood. From day one, it was clear that our Puerto Rican neighbors would always be very good neighbors and very good friends, and nothing at all, from that point on, has changed my opinion about that.

There is more to say about the neighborhood's demographics, but before that, it might be worth it to know a little bit about the neighborhood's physical layout. It could have not been better configured and located for parents looking for an ideal place to live and raise a family. I do not know how my parents found it, but they scored with it in a very big way.

In somewhat of a sunken urban valley that Amsterdam Avenue, Broadway, and LaSalle Street spill down into, technically speaking, our new housing complex is not in Harlem; it is actually in Morningside Heights. The short stretch of 125th Street next to my building is one of the borders that divide these two sections, and we lived just inside the Morningside Heights dividing line. Then too, in some ways, our section of Morningside Heights is like a small subset of Harlem at the same time. Now sometimes called "So-Ha," an acronym for South of Harlem, there is a thin and hazy borderline that divides these two sections on the upper west side of Manhattan. With that being the case, no one could have convinced us that we didn't live in Harlem. Then too just as well, we had the heart, soul, and spirit of Harlem, Morningside Heights, and Spanish Harlem all rolled into one. So we were unique in that we had a bit of all three of these different and interesting worlds.

The ground floor lobbies of our buildings have six large apartments for the largest families. Two front doors lead to an open area with a canopy that provides cover from rain, snow, and heat from the direct sunlight. Since "loitering" was not permitted in either of these areas, we avoided standing there for too long. Those areas were like the three-second lane on a basketball court, and we knew, all too well, that if we lingered there for too long, one of the housing guards or police officers would appear from out of nowhere reaching for his citation pad to cite us for loitering. On the other hand, when it rained, the general assumption was that the no-loitering rule did not apply. So on rainy days, everyone gathered under the canopy to talk, play, or determine the best time to dash out into the rain to catch a bus, or go to the store without being cited.

On the left side of the canopy there is a ramp that leads to the Amsterdam Avenue side, and an elongated concrete set of stairs leads to the very popular 125th Street on the right side. Essentially, the ramp leads to Morningside Heights and the stairs leads to Harlem. So, right at our front doors, we had pathways leading to each section. Without a doubt, one could be no more Harlem than 125th Street, and as well could be no more Morningside Heights than Amsterdam Avenue and LaSalle Street. In front of the building was a large playground that had a lawn surrounding it. Then just beyond that is the very busy Amsterdam Ave. and 125th St. intersection. This is another point where Harlem and Morningside Heights meet, both geographically and culturally. The playground had monkey bars, a maze-like wooden corral, and three large concrete barrels we could climb on, or crawl around inside of. They were perfect for two games we played called "Johnny rides the pony" and "flies up." We also passed the time sitting in these barrels on rainy days. There was a long and slightly curved line of benches just beyond the building's canopy, and two shorter benches at the yard's periphery that were perfect for enjoying warm summer nights outdoors.

Across the street on the Harlem side there was a row of tenement apartment buildings. Then too, at the street level there was the K&K grocery store. This was where we did our day-to-day food shopping. The store was owned by two brothers whose last name was Kline. Not only was it conveniently located, but the Kline brothers allowed people to buy food on credit. They even hired kids to do deliveries for them. The K&K market was an old-fashioned neighborhood grocery store where the scent of food hung prominently and appetizingly in the air. For being such a small store, they were well stocked at all times, and they always had whatever we needed. Though well stocked, milk was the one thing that we didn't have to buy there in most cases; we had a milkman who delivered ice-cold bottles of milk to our doors two or three times a week, and, as far as I know, not as much as one bottle was ever borrowed, stolen, or "accidentally" misplaced; that was simply the way we were, and how we lived.

The K&K Market closed at 6 o'clock, but only a few doors away was another old-fashioned mom and pop styled grocery store that stayed open until 11 o'clock, called "Charlie's." Charlie was a Chinese man who always chewed on an unlit cigar. Groucho Marx and his ever-present stogie had nothing on Charlie. An inch-long piece of ash always hung precariously at the end of his cigars while he waited on his customers, and I do not ever remember seeing his cigars lit, or seeing the ashes fall off. Charlie's wife was usually busy at the back end of the store while his daughter pitched in to help Charlie with customers at the front counter. I might add that this was long before the bulletproof fiberglass partitions that have become fixtures in so many corner grocery stores. Then too, even without these partitions, I never once heard of any kind of crime taking place at any of our neighborhood stores or other commercial establishments.

Along with Charlie's ubiquitous cigar, one other thing that was always present and noticeable was the firearm strapped to Charlie's hip, and under his jacket. Though we always felt comfortable around Charlie, to see someone other than a police officer with a firearm was sobering to say the least. Though there was never a time when he had to use his weapon, somehow I had the clear impression that someone would have had a big problem on their hands had they chosen to tangle with Charlie.

On that same block were two Latin-American styled grocery stores called bodegas. Though Puerto Rican families did their shopping at the bodegas primarily, many of the curious African-American kids did not hesitate buying and sampling the different food items sold there. We used to buy sugar cane stalks, peel off the skin, cut the stalks into inch-long pieces, and chew on them. We also used to buy and eat the small green pieces of fruit called quenepas (in Puerto Rico) or mamoncillos (in Cuba).

One very popular item sold at the bodegas and from pushcarts on the street was something called piraguas, or icees. Made of shaved ice placed inside a paper cone, the ice is covered with a fruit-flavored syrup of one's choice: grape, coconut, orange, pineapple, cherry, and more. The mound of ice has a cone shape that looks like a pyramid. The vendors pressed a funnel down onto the ice to give it its perfect shape. Piraguas got its name by combining the Spanish words for pyramid and water. Costing only ten cents, they were inexpensive and refreshing treats on hot summer days.

Like piraguas, the ice-cold beer sold at the bodegas was another item that hardly went unnoticed. The bodegas had a knack for putting a chill on a can of beer that could not be beat. The shards of ice floating in each can were testaments to this fact, and that made their beer the best beer on the block, as I learned much later. During the summer months of my teenage beer-drinking phase, a "cold one" from one of our bodegas and a bag of "Wise" potato chips made sitting outside and chatting with my friends even more fun. Additionally, these Latin-American grocery stores added another nice feeling of barrio and diversity to the neighborhood, and we had four or five bodegas in the general area.

Midway between Charlie's and K & K was Frank's Liquor Store. As I mentioned, its bright red and green sign flashed and reflected up and onto the ceiling of my bedroom at night. Right next to Frank's was a candy store that we called Mr. Eddie's. Mr. Eddie's was another small but compact store, and he sold just about anything a kid could want. Along with the barbershop (where men played "the numbers" by poking their heads in the door to flash hand signals, or call out the 3-digit numbers indicating the horse-racing results for the hour), Mr. Eddie was one of the two African-American merchants in the neighborhood, and he indeed got his share of the neighborhood's business given the many items he sold to us sugar fueled, fun-loving children. Candy, comic books, sodas, potato chips, ice cream, model airplanes, spinning tops, jump ropes, yo-yos, pumpkinseeds, bubblegum, baseball cards, newspapers, games, and toys could all be found at Mr. Eddie's small and compact candy store.

Rounding out the remaining assortment of stores and business establishments on this block-long stretch of 125th Street there was a bakery, two bars, a pet shop, a paper goods store, a barbershop, a hardware store, a dry cleaners, a pizza parlor, a newspaper stand, and a discount clothing store (called Fella's Department Store where we all shopped [at one time or another], but no one would ever say that they did). The same was true with John's Bargain Store on the other side of Amsterdam Avenue. With this array of business establishments, anything we needed was within a short and careful walk across the busy roadway popularly known as 125th Street (at that time). Then too, along with this cluster of stores and other business establishments there was even more.

There is another stretch of stores and commercial establishments on 125th Street, just east of Morningside Heights that is Harlem's economic heartbeat. This, perhaps, mile-long stretch of 125th Street cuts across Harlem from Morningside Avenue to First Avenue on the east side. Along this commercial stretch there were movie theaters, restaurants, banks, shoe stores, office buildings, hotels, department stores, food markets, a post office, jewelry stores, pawn shops, record stores, clothing stores, street vendors, a musical instrument store, a sporting goods store, a dental office, a penny arcade, a bicycle store, places to eat, bars, a fire station, the Baby Grand Jazz Club, and just about anything else you can think of. Legal and (sometimes) not so legal street vendors sold items from tables or while they walked up and down the long and busy Harlem thoroughfare. One guy sold watches, and chanted the same thing all the time: "Don't ask me where I get them from!" This was his slogan and the hook that he used humorously to catch people's attention.

During the Christmas Holidays, the merchants of 125th St. strung Christmas lights along the popular promenade, and we had a perfect view of it from our living room window. It is a spectacular lighting display that added (and still adds) something special to the Christmas Holidays and to the neighborhood.

Then in the middle of it all is the Apollo Theater. This, without a doubt, is Harlem's epicenter, and we were fortunate enough to have moved to a building that was only three blocks from this world-renowned entertainment venue. Now, more than ever, I realize how lucky I was to have moved to a neighborhood that has played host to so many great recording artists and comedians. With a casual stroll down 125th Street on any given day, my friends and I saw the names of such greats as Aretha Franklin, The Temptations, Moms Mabley, Marvin Gaye, Wilson Pickett, The Shirelles, Diana Ross and the Supremes, Redd Foxx, Stevie Wonder, Smokey Robinson and The Miracles, James Brown, and more on the Apollo's marquee.

Whenever James Brown played at the Apollo Theater, everyone knew about it long before his opening night. The Record Shack and all of the other record stores on 125th Street placed James Brown's album covers on display in their windows and blasted his music from speakers in front of the stores well ahead of his arrival. Then on the nights of his performances, lines of people circled the block (often in sub-freezing weather) waiting to get in to see "The Godfather of Soul." It seemed as if James Brown owned 125th Street during his weeklong appearances.

The Theresa Hotel was on Seventh Avenue, between 124th and 125th Streets, just down the block and across the street from the Apollo Theater, and I think this was where the Apollo's performing artists stayed during their Apollo engagements. It was the largest and most popular hotel in Harlem. When Fidel Castro came to New York City to address the United Nations' General Assembly in 1960, the hotel's name recognition was catapulted onto the world stage. After hitting a snag of red tape and being snubbed by city officials and the Midtown hotel establishment, Fidel Castro and his entourage came to Harlem and stayed at the Theresa Hotel. When the press heard about it, they asked him if he was concerned about having to stay in Harlem. He told them that he was not concerned at all and added that they could pitch tents and sleep in Central Park if necessary. Then he told them that he looked forward to getting to know Harlem and its people. I do not know what the press had to say about his visit and reply, but it all went over very well with many of Harlem's residents. So despite the fuss his visit to New York City caused, a surprisingly large number of people responded favorably to his impromptu stay and gracious words.

Marred by our own negative press, it was considered a feather in our cap to have such a prominent world figure stay in our neighborhood.

Harlem and my neighborhood played host to another dignitary when former President John F. Kennedy visited. In his large motorcade, he rode right down the middle of 125th Street in an open convertible smiling and waving to the large crowd that turned out to greet him. They passed right by my building, and my family and I were able to see him very well from my bedroom window as he looked up and waved to everyone.

All of that and more were on the Harlem side of our building, but there was still more on the Morningside Heights side. On Amsterdam Avenue there was another collection of high-rise apartment buildings called the Morningside Gardens Co-ops. Though the Morningside Heights Gardens Co-ops look a lot like our buildings, it does not take long to see that they are several cuts above our lower-income/working-class section of the neighborhood. Despite that fact, "Grant" was rich in spirit, and we sizzled with activity, culture, and diversity.

At the ground floor level there was a large supermarket that was called "the Co-ops." This was where we did our Saturday morning food shopping. On the same block there was a stationary/candy store, a drugstore, a diner, a Chinese restaurant, a delicatessen, and a Japanese gift shop that sold candy that was wrapped in rice paper that we were all fascinated by. The rice paper looked like clear cellophane, but it dissolved once we popped the unwrapped candy into our mouths and started to chew. So we had the unusual thrill of eating candy without unwrapping the paper around it. Rounding out the immediate area, there were lines of additional business establishments branching out from the Amsterdam Ave. and 125th St. intersection in all four directions.

With all that our new neighborhood had to offer, it is also directly or indirectly associated with several people of note. The first African-American justice of the Supreme Court, Thurgood Marshall, lived in the Morningside Gardens Co-ops. As well did singer and songwriter Fiona Apple and novelist Robert Crichton. George Carlin, the brilliant comedian and actor grew up only a few blocks away from my building on 121st Street between Broadway and Amsterdam Avenue. I saw recently that the street was named in his honor, and it is now called George Carlin Way. In an interview, I heard him say he was from Morningside Heights. Then, jokingly, he cleared his throat and called it "White Harlem." I heard Aerosmith's front man and singer, Steven Tyler, say that he lived near the Apollo Theater. R&B singer, Keith Sweat, is from building 430 in our very own Grant Housing complex. I understand that Mick Jagger was an occasional visitor to our neighborhood too. When James Brown and his review played at the Apollo Theater, Mick Jagger was right there to catch his performances. Nedra Talley lived in building 1305. She sang with her two cousins Veronica (a.k.a. Ronnie Spector) and Estelle Bennett in the popular "girl" singing group of the early 60s called the Ronettes. The Ronettes are known widely for their hit tune, "Be My Baby." Then in building 75 LaSalle Street, in "Grant," is where Sylvia Peterson lived, and she sang with the Chiffons. The Chiffons were well known for their hit tune, "He's So Fine." Sylvia's younger sister, Francine, was one of my many childhood friends. Then for basketball fans and historians, another childhood friends of mine from Grant named Raymond Dalmau coached the Puerto Rican National Olympic Basketball Team, and he lived at 75 LaSalle Street too. While watching the Puerto Rican basketball team play the 1992 U.S. Olympic Dream Team on television, I was pleasantly surprised when the camera focused in on Raymond while he huddled with his team during a timeout. Well known and much appreciated for his accomplishments as a player, a sports arena in Quebradillas, Puerto Rico was named in his honor. He holds a prestigious scoring record, by scoring 11,000 points during the time he played with the popular Puerto Rican team, Los Piratas de Quebradillas; and I understand that he scored 115 points in a single game back during that time. Then too like all of us, he learned to play basketball on our Morningside Heights and Harlem playgrounds. The multi-talented Ricardo Marrero was a good friend of mine, and he lived and grew up in Grant too. He has played keyboard and several other instruments for Ruben Blades and his band, Seis del Solar. Additionally, Eddy Zervigon, the brilliant and distinguished Cuban flute player who founded and directs Orquesta Broadway lived just north of Morningside Heights, and only ten blocks from our immediate neighborhood.

The chances were good that Wilt Chamberlain lived somewhere nearby too, or was, at least, a regular visitor to the neighborhood. Though I never saw him, stories about Wilt Chamberlain sightings were frequent. He regularly visited a popular Harlem nightclub, and as urban legend has it, the nightclub was called Big Wilt's Small Paradise because Wilt Chamberlain spent so much time there. Wilt Chamberlain was another basketball player who created a stir by scoring 100 points in a single basketball game against the New York Knicks. It was in bold print in the New York Daily News the next day, and everyone talked about it for the longest time. Wilt Chamberlain created another stir by the way he scooted around in his Volkswagen Bug or his white Cadillac. The stories usually had to do with seeing him squeeze his 7-feet 1-inch frame in and out of his flashy cars. Cuban novelist, Oscar Hijuelos, was a resident of Morningside Heights. He was the first Latin American author to win a Pulitzer Prize for his book (and eventual movie) "Mambo Kings Play Songs of Love." Dizzy Gillespie's niece lived in Grant too. Her name is Carol, and like Francine, Richie, and Raymond, she is a childhood friend of mine too. I had the pleasure of chatting with her comical and good-natured uncle at one of his performances, and I told him that I know and grew up with his niece.

With one caveat I'd say that the chances are good that jazz drummer Al Foster lived somewhere in the neighborhood too, and I am pretty sure we went to the same junior high school. While returning to class after lunch one day, a group of us were stopped in our tracks as we listened to an outstanding drum solo coming from the school's auditorium. Given what we heard, it was clear that the drummer was bound for great things. So I made it a point to remember his name after hearing it mentioned several times while we listened to him play. Then years later I learned that someone named Al Foster played drums for Miles Davis. Al Foster was born in Richmond, Virginia, but I understand that he grew up in NYC. Though I cannot say conclusively that it is the same person, all evidence seems to indicate that it is the same Al Foster, unless there are two or more exceptional drummers from Harlem named Al Foster.

In a slightly different take on this who's who of the neighborhood, this one, in particular, has to do with composer, pianist, and songstress Alicia Keys. Though she was born and raised in the Hell's Kitchen section of Manhattan, the video for her song, "If I Ain't Got You," was shot in our neighborhood. I didn't realize it at first, but after getting a better look at the all too familiar backdrop and the positioning of Grant's tall brick buildings in the background, I recorded it, played it back, slowed it down, and paused it for a better look. Then (in the video) when I saw her walking down a flight of stairs in Morningside Park, and saw a quick shot of 125th Street's 8th Avenue train station entrance, I knew I had it right. This song has always been one of my favorites, but I liked it even more after realizing that the video for it was shot in our neighborhood. There are several oldies that have a way of taking me back to the old neighborhood whenever I hear them: Under the Boardwalk, On Broadway, and Spanish Harlem are perfect examples of this. They never fail to evoke fond memories of the Coney Island Boardwalk, Spanish Harlem, and the section of Broadway that passes through our neighborhood. Be that as it may, in terms of a more contemporary song that does the same thing for me, this song by Alicia Keys captures the neighborhood for me in every way. I don't know what went into her choosing that area for her video's location, given the many places there are to choose from. Whatever it was, it speaks volumes to the beauty and character of this part of NYC, Harlem, and Morningside Heights. So I think her choice was a very good one. Additionally, given that I have seen the neighborhood as much as I do in films and in music videos, clearly, it is a popular location for film directors and recording artists. Then certainly last but not least, Jay Z and Alicia Key's classic, Empire State of Mind, not only takes me back to the old neighborhood, but it so well captures growing up, and living in New York City.

The four buildings on our side of Amsterdam Ave. are on a block the size of four city blocks. It extends east and west from Amsterdam Ave. to

Morningside Ave, and north and south from 125th St. to 123rd St. The block is large enough for each building to have its own large playground in front. There are two parking lots, and Grant's Community Center is right behind my buildings. Our new elementary school, P.S.125, is on the same block too. Along with the school building, there is a large schoolyard complex with an area for softball, basketball, handball, and an additional play area for small children. The block has areas with large patches of grass and trees, and a paved pathway cuts a winding swath through the area that gives quick and easy access to any part of the neighborhood. These pathways eventually became perfect for the many enthusiastic skaters and bicyclist who soon made their presence known.

The other block is the same size, and it has the same unusual shape as ours. It has a public library, more yards, lawns, two parking lots, paved pathways, and its own assortment of stores and commercial establishments. At the Broadway and 125th Street intersection are the entrances to the very popular elevated Broadway and 125th Street train station. Then on the other side of Broadway is another neighborhood called Tiemann Place. This was where the bulk of our Italian neighbors, schoolmates, and friends lived. Tiemann Place has more tenement walk-ups and another wide variety of stores and commercial establishments, including our favorite place for a tasty bite to eat at Maria's Pizzeria.

Given the location of our beautiful 15-acre urban village, its 1,940 apartments, and the many surrounding neighborhoods, I was hardly limited to the 226 apartments of my building when it came to finding and meeting new friends. Though this kind of population density does not work for everyone, I loved it. People were everywhere; and our new neighborhood hummed and vibrated with a level of vitality far beyond anything our old neighborhood had on its best days. As kids, we could have not asked for more when it came to having a great neighborhood to grow up in and live.

Given the African, southern, northeastern, and urban influences that made us who we were, the African-American residents of the neighborhood made for some pretty fun and interesting people too. Living among so many interesting people has left its mark on me forever, and the experience was a very good one for me. As we grew up and lived together over the years, we melded into one big family. We looked out for each other in the same way we looked out for our own family members. And in the southern tradition of our parents, we greeted friends and neighbors warmly while passing on the street. The present-day, tragic, and infectious epidemic of funky attitudes, sideways glances, shading, ghosting, and the like were not things that we ascribed to. We took a dim view of any kind of vapid self-centered behavior like that. Integrity, character, and civility was what we made a habit of practicing, and anything less than that was seen as nothing for us to strive for or imitate. As always, there are exceptions to just about everything, but those who felt a need to carry themselves in less than that way were few and far between. I hasten to add that this sense of family and community very much included the Puerto Rican people, too. We looked out for them, and they looked out for us in a commendable way; we were all one big family-like community.

Whatever the personality type or the individual interests, friendships were formed instantly and have remained intact to this day. Over the last thirty years or more, our neighborhood has hosted an annual Father's Day gathering where hundreds of people from the neighborhood come together for a block-party styled reunion. At these reunions, we spend the day reminiscing, reconnecting, eating, listening to music, and catching up on what we have been doing in our various walks of life.

I would be remiss not to mention that our neighborhood was endowed with an assortment of some pretty striking females. Given their sense of dignity, identity, intelligence, humor, warmth, and zest for life, they added something extra special to our exceptional urban village. Guys from all over New York City and Harlem came to our neighborhood, regularly, for this very reason. So like clockwork, when the winter months gave way to spring and summer, a procession of females kicked in that we guys knew all too well. As sad as it was for me to leave Hamilton Heights, after getting a look at this new and diverse assortment of girls, the move did not seem to be such a bad deal to me after all; and there is little that I can think of that could have convinced me to leave.

As we ventured out to meet the kids from the other buildings, there were no territorial disputes, or infighting that sometimes divides African-American people and communities, we were more than happy to meet and learn about each other. Without a doubt, we did have our few scoundrels who regularly looked for some kind of mischief to get themselves into. The least of which were those who got some kind of a cheap thrill from throwing water balloons out of their windows or pushing all of the elevator buttons before getting off the elevator. By doing this, the next rider would have the time of his or her elevator ride increased, given that the elevator stopped at each floor. So depending on which floor the next rider lived, what should have been a one-minute ride could have taken as long as ten. Nevertheless, with the fine job done by our conscientious parents, the overwhelming majority of us were very good kids, and we were able to bond in a very special way.

Though the hallways leading to our apartments were no more than five-feet wide, they were perhaps one hundred feet long. From the second floor up, the hallways were practically identical. So, if someone did not pay attention to the number markings on the elevator doors, he or she could unwittingly get off the elevator on the wrong floor and have to walk up or down several flights of stairs to get home. Even more unsettling than that, and as I'd done two or three times, someone could get off the elevator on the wrong floor, go to the wrong apartment door, rattle their key in someone else's lock, frustratingly shake the door, and wonder why it would not open. Then, if they were lucky enough to realize their mistake in time, they might have had enough time to make a quick getaway before someone came to the door to investigate the disturbance.

Along with the eleven apartments on each floor, there were two doors that led to our two elevators, and two staircases that could be used in emergency situations. On each floor there was a long and coiled fire hose that could reach any apartment. Then to the left of the elevator doors was a small maintenance supply closet and an incinerator hatch door against the wall. Along with that, Grant's maintenance crew did an excellent job of sweeping and mopping each of the 21 floors of our hallways once a week.

Given the way that New York City and Harlem have changed over the years, whenever I hear people talk about returning to their old neighborhoods, invariably they speak sadly of how much everything has changed. Not only are they unable to find former neighbors, or childhood friends, but they are not even able to find any old buildings or other familiar landmarks. But fortunately for us at "Grant," this is not the case; and I hope that Grant continues to be the special place that has marked the starting point for generations of fine, friendly, interesting, and hardworking people. Not only has the neighborhood's appearance hardly changed, but there are still people living there who I can visit. Presently, on any given day, in the sea of unfamiliar faces, I can expect to see someone I know walking by within a matter of minutes.

As I took in the sights and sounds of our new neighborhood, I had no idea that our beautiful hamlet would be shaken by a catastrophe that dashed the hopes and dreams of some truly remarkable people. Though this happened several years after we moved in, we were on a collision course with a fate that hit us like a tidal wave. As it did with the rest of Harlem and much of the NYC area, it marred and drastically changed the course of our neighborhood's history forever.

Nevertheless, before this sad chapter, there was plenty of growing up and connecting with people to be done. During these first few summer months, our outdoor activities were limited to the front yards of our buildings. So we did not meet the kids from the other buildings until school started in the fall. In the meantime, the girls played hopscotch and double Dutch, and we guys spun spinning tops, slung yo-yos, skated, played punch ball, loadies, and all kinds of other games to keep ourselves entertained.

At the end of our summer break, my brother started the first grade and my sister and I started the fourth. Our new elementary school, P.S. 125, separated my sister and me by putting us in different classes for some reason. At P.S. 46 we were always in the same class, and we always had the same teachers. My fourth grade teacher's name was Mrs. Thomason, and my sister's teacher's name was Mrs. Valdez. Since our new school was on our block, those of us who lived on our side of Amsterdam Avenue did not have to cross one street of automobile traffic shuttling ourselves to and from school every day.

Before P.S. 125 became a public school, it was a private school. So there were some special things that came with going to school there. We had a full-sized swimming pool, a woodshop, a boys' and girls' gymnasium, an auditorium, an elevator, a large outdoor yard complex, an annex to the main building, and a rooftop playground. Our student body was largely African-American and Puerto Rican, but a handful of Italian, Korean, Jewish, Irish, Japanese, and Chinese kids attended P.S. 125 too; and though there was no way for us to fully appreciate the experience at that age, just like our neighborhood, our school provided us with a priceless education about people and the larger world around us.

On the first day of school Mrs. Thomason asked each of us to come to the front of the classroom to introduce ourselves. I do not remember my presentation, but it is likely that I spoke of being a Dodger fan or about my fondness for baseball. One student, to this day, always gets a good laugh whenever I remind him of his presentation. Then, as if baffled by the memory of it, he always asks me, "What made me do that?" When it was his turn, he strutted up to the front of the classroom wearing a bowtie and a crisp white shirt. He told us that his name is Steven Wright, and he told us that he wanted to sing a song for us. Then he launched himself, enthusiastically, into a spirited cowboy song that broke the ice and stole the show. When he finished singing, the entire class clapped, whooped, and hollered. Pleased with the response and the fine job he'd done, he proudly walked back to his desk with a smile that we all got to know all too well in the days, weeks, months, and years to come. Being the Yankee fan that Steven was at that time, and with the Yankees and the Braves locked in a heated race for the World Series that year, whenever we sang the Star Spangled Banner, he had his own version. At the part of the song where we sang: "O'er the land of the free and the home of the brave," Steven had his own version, he would sing: "O'er the land of the free and the home of the Yankees," and would then flash his enthusiastic smile.

With a curriculum that included the usual elementary school subjects, we had woodshop, music, physical education, and swimming. Our woodshop teacher, Mr. Henderson, did an excellent job of teaching us how to use the heavy-duty equipment without lopping off any fingers or boring holes into our hands with the high-speed drills and electric saws. The music teacher, Mr. Booth, taught me to play the French horn, drums, and eventually the recorder; and my sister played the autoharp. We were given sheet music, and were taught to read standard musical notation. Then, it was not long before we had a small collection of songs we were able to play. The first song I learned on the recorder was a Mexican song called Cielito Lindo (Beautiful Little Sky). In Spanish the word sky, "cielo," is also used affectionately for a loved one. Playing the recorder and learning music theory became valuable gifts that have served me well over the years. On Saturdays, Chinese classes were provided for those of us who were interested, and we learned to speak, write, and read Chinese characters. Then too, on Thursdays we were able to ditch school for the afternoon to attend religious instruction at Corpus Cristi Church on 121st Street. This was on George Carlin's block, and Corpus Cristi Church was the Catholic school that George Carlin attended.

Although we had a swimming pool at P.S. 125, no one taught us how to swim during our swimming classes. So we were content playing and splashing around at the shallow end of the pool. Our pool was not heated, and we had to get into the pool's cold water once a week regardless of how cold the weather was outside. Making matters worse, we had to take showers in water that was colder than the pool's water. These ice cold showers were torture, and I will never know why we were subjected to something so unpleasant. Despite having to take these cold showers, it did make getting into the pool's cold water a lot easier. After one of those ice-cold showers, the pool's water actually felt warm by comparison. Though it was much later when I learned to swim, by having this head start, I had long overcome any fear I had of the water.

Mrs. Thomason told us once that our brains would rust if we don't use them. I remember trying very hard to imagine what brain rust looks like, but realized much later that she was speaking metaphorically.

During the summer break and before moving on to the fifth grade, with a quickly widening collection of friends and a better feel for the neighborhood, a magnetic pull drew us guys to our school's softball field. There, I realized that I was not the only baseball fanatic in the neighborhood. Because my father was always there in support, and so willing to lend a helping hand to the other kids, he quickly became popular with the kids from the neighborhood.

At the schoolyard, we met a man named Leroy Otis. Leroy was a coach and one of Harlem's great sports and coaching legends. Be it baseball, softball, basketball, or football he was very good at finding kids and molding them into winning teams. He loved coaching, and the various merchants and organizations in the neighborhood financed his one-man coaching operation. As a result, he had equipment, jerseys, and caps for all of us.

Leroy's entire life seemed to be devoted to sports, coaching, and kids. He came to the softball field to talk and joke with us every Saturday morning. I never knew where he was from, but his accent was a clear indicator that he was from somewhere in the South; and the kids loved to tease him about it. Leroy had a habit of jingling what seemed like a small fortune of loose change in his hands and pockets. In spite of his generosity as a coach and otherwise, we did learn quickly that he was the wrong person to ask if we were looking for a loan or handout of some kind. After one or two attempts, we knew all too well that it would lead to nothing more than a lecture on the folly of poor money management. So it was clear, early on, that asking Leroy for money was not worth the bother. I realize, now, that he didn't have much of a choice in the matter; there were just too many kids around him to let the word get out that he was a soft touch for money.

One day I heard one of the kids from Leroy's older division team ask him how was his lip feeling, and then he started to laugh after asking him. In reply, Leroy told him that he didn't think what they did was all that funny. One of the kids pushed a harmless (candy store) exploding wick into the front end of one of Leroy's cigarettes when he wasn't looking. Then later when Leroy reached to light up to enjoy a smoke (after dealing with us kids all day), he had the shock of his life when the front end of his cigarette exploded. Had it been any other coach, heads would have likely rolled that day, but Leroy was not that type of coach or person. He knew kids, and more than that he loved coaching; and he was devoted to shaping kids into good athletes and fine human beings.

Before long, Leroy had us out on the softball field every Saturday morning working on fundamentals as he molded us into a powerhouse of a softball team. Then he placed us in softball leagues to compete with other teams from Harlem and teams from NYC's Police Athletic League (PAL). I played on two of his teams. One team was called St. Joseph's and the other one was the Lucas Electrical Company, a church and an electrical supply store in the neighborhood.

Steven Wright played centerfield. William Hines played leftfield. Embrit Joynes played rightfield, Walter Toomer was at shortstop, James Harvey was our second baseman, Clyde Brenner was at third base, Benny Wright was our catcher, James Crane, Melvin Nelson, and Perry Elliott shared the pitching position, and I played first base.

I was not much of a hitter, but with my right foot on first base, I knew how to stretch out my long arm and legs to catch any ball thrown to me to retire the base runner trying to beat out a groundball and the play at first base. I would have been a much better hitter had I done a better job of keeping my eyes on the ball. I realized this many years later when a friend taught me to play tennis and emphasized how important this metaphor is for so much of what we do in life. Wanting so much to get a good and solid hit, I had a bad habit of closing my eyes or taking my eyes off the ball when I swung. This usually resulted in me slicing the ball into a pop-up or striking out. At best, I would get lucky sometimes, connect, and tap a few pitches into the outfield for a single. But more than anything I wanted to experience the thrill of blasting one over the fence and out of the park, and then watch my teammates go crazy with celebration as I made my way around the bases and back to home plate.

We were a pretty lively crew at our Saturday morning practices. The popping sound of the ball slamming into our leather gloves echoed loudly around the schoolyard as we tried to knock the gloves off of each other's hands. From the moment we hit the field, Leroy would have a nonstop monologue going for the entire length of our practice sessions while he barked out instructions and words of encouragement to us.

Leroy wanted no part of a lethargic or lackadaisical team. So if he thought for a second that we were only going through the motions without the enthusiasm he liked to see, he would start in on us right away: "Ok, let's go, let's go! Let's talk it up out there guys; let's talk it up! Let's get after that "bawl" (ball) gentlemens!" Then if a ground ball got away and rolled between the feet of one of our infielders, Leroy would usually have something to say about it: "You better check to see if you got a hole in that glove there fella, letting an easy groundball get away from you like that!" Spectators gathered around the outside of the softball field to watch us. Hearing the buzz and excitement coming from the crowd was inspiring, and it made me feel as if I were a part of a major league baseball team.

Leroy stood in the batter's box with a bat in his right hand resting on his shoulder and a ball in his left hand. He would toss the ball about four feet into the air, slice at it, and tap it to whomever he wanted. If he called for a double play before hitting a groundball between second and third base, Walter would scoop it up, throw it to James at second base, and James would throw it to me at first base as we simulated a double play. I would then throw the ball to the catcher, and we quickly moved the ball around the infield trying to get the loudest pop from our gloves to add to the excitement and to keep everyone involved as much as possible.

Across the street from our softball field was Morningside Park. Morningside Park extends lengthwise from 123rd Street down to 110th Street. When the snow fell, Morningside Park became a winter wonderland and was perfect for snowball fights, riding sleds, cardboard boxes, or anything else we could find to slide down its snow-covered hills on. In the summer, the park exploded with lush green trees and grass. Additionally, Morningside Park has basketball courts and a small dirt and grassy area where we played pickup games of hardball. There were two very nice baseball diamonds at the southern end of Morningside Park where we played our summer-league games.

After our pre-game practice drills, Leroy would call us together into a circle at the middle of the infield. Then very seriously and with every bit of his southern accent supporting his words, he would always start his pep talks the same way: "Now listen gentlemens, for your information…" He would then pass on any of his thoughts to us regarding our progress as a team, what we needed to work on, and how important the day's game was. Then at the end of one of these pep talks, we would be ready to play. I do not remember what our overall won-loss record was, but we had plenty of trophies to show for our many championship wins.

This was my first experience with any kind of organized sports, and it was a very good lesson for me about teamwork, sportsmanship, and working as a group for a common goal. More than just the fun of playing a game I loved, I learned plenty of valuable lessons that I would carry with me from that point on. As a coach, a friend, or someone to just sit around and talk to, Leroy Otis gave us so much through sports.

After what seemed like an endless summer of fun and good times, it was time for me to start the fifth grade. Despite the summer fun, I liked the idea of returning to school in the fall. Buying school supplies and the anticipation of doing schoolwork again were things that I looked forward to. However, in spite of my enthusiasm, the fifth grade was the first time I found myself struggling with schoolwork. It felt to me as if I'd hit a brick wall. As the work became more challenging, it became increasingly difficult for me to grasp things that should have not presented me with so many problems. As I struggled, it started to erode both my enthusiasm and confidence. As I sank more and more into this listless quagmire, school and learning soon became much less than the enjoyable process that it should have been for me.

Making matters worse, I had formed the habit of daydreaming while in class. Very often, I would become so overtaken by one of my vivid daydreams that I would have no idea of how long I'd been staring into space, completely oblivious to the fact that I was in a classroom with a lesson underway, once I finally snapped out of it. Then after tuning back into the classroom proceedings and hearing the teacher drone on for another minute or two, I would soon be off again to some other distant place. The teacher knew it, and loved to catch me or any other "daydreamer" off guard. He would do this by loudly and clearly tacking our names on to the tail end of a question about the lesson. After missing the question, and then hearing my name, I was not even able to fake an answer. Then there would be a long, loud, awkward, and embarrassing silence.

The same thing happened to me while reading. With a book right in front of me, my mind would wander off and return later leaving me frustrated at my inability to hold a steady line of focus. Then when it came to math, things were not any better. Through no one's fault other than my own and for no reason that I can explain, I would not and could not muster what I needed to memorize all of the times tables. I had a mental block or a level of apathy that prevented me from memorizing the six, seven, eight, and nine-times tables. Hence, I did no better when it came to division and fractions. Be it math, reading, or our writing exercises, I seemed to almost always find myself on the wrong page. So I would have been the perfect poster child for attention deficit disorder. I don't know what it was with my brain wiring; I was intrigued by schoolwork, studying, and learning, but when it came to getting it done I could never seem to find my footing; and it was very frustrating for me.

Further complicating matters was the fact that the fifth grade was the first time I had ever seen kids who were bold enough to defy a teacher with any class clown antics. I was not disruptive; that was not the type of kid I was. Besides that, I would have to have plenty of explaining to do if my mother heard about me doing anything like that. Learning difficulties was one thing, but unacceptable behavior in class was something else; and my mother had no tolerance for it. But because clowning was now a part of the classroom proceedings, it only added a distraction that I hardly needed. Due to Mrs. Thomason's iron-fisted rule, we all knew not to even think of trying it with her.

I saw her response to a disciplinary matter once, and came dangerously close to being on its receiving end. Mrs. Thomason needed to clean out a small colony of roaches that made their way into a small area behind a wall at the back of our classroom. In order to give herself time to get it done, she gave us an assignment to do quietly while she cleaned. While we worked, a kid sitting at the desk next to mine started to talk to me, thinking he was clear of Mrs. Thomason's eyesight and earshot. It was a good thing that I didn't say anything to him, because Mrs. Thomason (despite her age) was on him as quickly and quietly as a cat. Then with an insecticide-soaked, and roach-covered rag (without saying a word), she swatted him across the top of his head with it, leaving several dead roaches falling down onto his shoulders, chest, and lap. So with her sharp eyes and ears, she knew exactly who was talking, and fortunately for me, I did not catch her archaic, harsh, and punitive response.

A teacher named Mrs. Allen was another heavy-handed disciplinarian at P.S. 125. She reminded me of a shark by the way she silently and chillingly glided through the hallway with her eyes darting around trying to catch someone breaking one of the rules. She saw me talking while I stood in line one day; then she crept up behind me, and pulled me out of line by my ear. I heard my ear crackling with sounds that I never knew were possible by pulling a human ear. The truth of the matter is that I am lucky that my ear was not permanently injured or disfigured by what she did. She was particularly brazen, and during my three years at P.S. 125 she never as much as said a word to me; she would not even nod to say hello when I passed her in the hallway. She had an eerie way of looking right through me as if I were not even there. The only time I had a sense that she knew I existed was when she had me by one of my ears. She didn't even say anything to me when she pulled me out of line. So that was my only interaction with the not so warm and fuzzy Mrs. Allen. If Mrs. Allen had the slightest hint or hunch that someone was goofing off in the boys' bathroom, she would transform herself into a one-woman SWAT team. Then, without warning, she would burst in to see what the problem was. With us boys standing at the urinals, we would be stunned to hear the door burst open violently and see Mrs. Allen standing there, glaring around angrily at everyone with one of her bone-chilling stares, looking like an ornery and crusty TV gunslinger from the wild-wild west. These days, a teacher would be in hot water for doing some of the things she did.

But Mrs. Allen and a few others took the liberty of using these extreme measures without fear of consequences back during that time. Not only that, but if any of us went home looking for sympathy from our parents, the chances were good that we would have been scolded again for breaking one of the rules.

My fifth grade teacher's name was Mr. Muslin, and his approach to disciplinary matters was better. He was a dead ringer for Superman's alter ego Clark Kent with his slicked back hair, prominent jaw-line, and large-framed eyeglasses. Under their breaths and behind his back, some of the kids called him Clark Kent. Mr. Muslin liked placing emphasis on art and culture. He taught us African, Jewish, and other songs from around the world. He even organized two plays that we did for our assembly. Mr. Muslin liked the way two kids and I slapped our hands against our legs and chests to create the rhythm for a song we sang called Hambone. He liked it enough to take us to a recording studio to record it one Saturday.

One day, a kid said something that landed him in hot water with Mr. Muslin. He was one of the budding class clowns that I spoke of, and I guess he thought that he would be able to get a laugh from the other kids with his comment. After Mr. Muslin said something to us about being Jewish, the kid said something that was a bit crude and in bad taste. I do not know how many people heard it, because no one laughed, and the room became uncomfortably silent. I heard it, and Mr. Muslin definitely heard it; and he did not appreciate it at all. He got up from his desk, walked towards the kid, and (at no more than a few inches away) told him that he would cut him down to size in a heartbeat for that comment if he were his age. The kid did not say a word and appeared to be just as startled by Mr. Muslin's reaction as we all were. When the tension from this episode subsided, it was clear that our startled classmate would not try to get a laugh with that ploy again; and this was my first clue that there was a type of discrimination that has nothing to do with skin color. After this brief but tense interlude, our school year was underway once again.

As I mentioned, my problems had to do with my inability to maintain any kind of sustained focus on my schoolwork. But when I did break one of the rules, I was held after class right along with any of the other habitual troublemakers to write about it. Instead of writing compositions about what we did or why we did it, we had to write the same sentence over and over again. So if we were talking in class without permission, we would have to write: "I must not talk in class without permission," 100 times, and sometimes more. There was one time that several of us had so many lines to write that we did not get out of school until 6 o'clock that evening, and Mr. Muslin gladly sat at his desk, doing his paperwork, until every line was completed and handed in. Fortunately for me, my parents were still at work when I returned, so they never knew anything about this unusually long detention. In hindsight, I know, now, how dedicated Mr. Muslin was, and how much he wanted to get the best from us. But, given the challenges that came with it, he did the best he could with what he knew.

As my academic free-fall continued, it was apparent on my report card. My grades were not looking good, and my mother was not happy about it at all. What was even more frustrating was the way that I could connect with my studies and bring my performance level up occasionally. Not only did it make my mother happy, but it made me feel good to see how much it pleased her. Then too, it made me feel good to feel the satisfaction that comes with applying myself more dedicatedly to my schoolwork. But these spurts of productivity were intermittent, and they would disappear as suddenly and as mysteriously as they had appeared. Then before long, I would be right back in the same old rut again, having little to no focus or enthusiasm for schoolwork.

Unable to sustain any kind of consistency, Mr. Muslin told me that I was at risk of being held back to repeat the fifth grade. My mother was frustrated, disappointed, and at her wits end with me. It was frustrating for me too, but I felt almost helpless to do anything about it. So at the end of a year of muddling through the fifth grade, Mr. Muslin told me that my work did not warrant me moving on to the sixth grade. Along with that bad news, he did offer me one option that would spare me the shame of having to repeat the fifth grade. He would allow me to go on to the sixth grade if, and only if, I completed a work assignment during the summer break.

With the summer being my time for fun, carefree, and easy living, schoolwork was the very last thing I wanted to spend my vacation time doing. But wanting no part of having to repeat the 5th grade, I had no choice but to forgo the first part of my summer break to get every last bit of my assignment done. The workload consisted of math, reading comprehension and writing. With some much needed help, I completed my assignment and was able to go on to the sixth grade. I owe so much to the daughter of one of my mother's best friends. Her name is Yvonne, and she pitched in to help me in my time of need. Mr. Muslin had piled the work on so high that I would have never gotten it done alone. Additionally, knowing that all of my friends were out and enjoying their summer vacations, it would have been a hopeless situation for me that was doomed for failure. Moreover, had I been forced to repeat the fifth grade, it would have caused me to miss out on an opportunity of a lifetime, that would have changed my life forever (as you will see later).

With my assignment completed, eventually I was able to get out to see my friends, get some fresh air and sunshine, and to have my first active introduction to basketball. So my summer of '59 was not a complete washout. As I mentioned, I saw kids playing basketball in Hamilton Heights before we moved. But given my blind devotion to baseball, basketball was something that I had never really thought about becoming involved with. But now, on P.S. 125's schoolyard, I was about to play my very first basketball game, without as much as ever touching a basketball. A group of kids, eager to get a pickup game started, needed another person to complete one of the two teams they were putting together. The one and only thing I knew about basketball was the rather obvious objective of scoring points by getting the ball into the basket; other than that I was clueless. I didn't know how to shoot, dribble, or any of the rules.

I told them that I didn't know how to play, but they didn't care. All they were interested in was getting another person on the court to get their game started, and since there was no one else available to play, I went high in this Harlem/Morningside Heights playground draft lottery. During the game, the ball finally ended up in my hands. After catching it, like a fullback on a football field, I took off running towards the basket without bouncing it once. The kids had a good laugh about it before telling me about dribbling, and how I needed to bounce the ball if I wanted to move around the court with it in my possession. They told me that moving both feet without bouncing the ball was a violation of one of the rules called "walking," and if I "walked" I would have to give the ball over to the other team. Then, for some reason, the game became interesting to me, and I liked basketball from that point on.

After one of my inexperienced shot attempts made for another round of laughter by clearing the entire rim and backboard by a good 6 feet, I was well on my way to learning how to play. The more I played, the more I learned, and the more I learned, the more I liked the game. My father bought a basketball for me, and I started to play under the hot sun for so long that I would be baked to a crisp by the end of the day. Then when I would finally tear myself away from the court to go home, there were a couple of times that my mother didn't even recognize me. Each time, she stood in the doorway with a puzzled look on her face until she realized it was me, her son, wanting to come into her house, several shades darker than I was when she saw me last.

With basketball being as popular as it is in Harlem and NYC, I started to play everyday. There were basketball courts everywhere, and everyone played. Between the schoolyard, P.S. 125's two gymnasiums, Teachers College, Stone Gym, and Morningside Park, basketball games went on practically around the clock. There were no basketball courts in our front yard, so we used the garbage cans, the monkey bars, cardboard boxes, and just about anything else we could think of to shoot a ball into. We even took turns standing with our fingers locked together forming a hoop with our arms while using our chest as the backboard. At home, my brother and I pulled the bottom section of a wire coat hanger down and placed the hook into the space at the top of our closed bedroom door. Then with a wadded up ball of socks or a Spalding punch ball, we played in our bedroom or hallway.

Along with the steady stream of pickup games that ended soon after it was too dark outside to see the ball or the basket, there was another basketball-related game we played just as enthusiastically that we called five-two. I am pretty sure that five-two is unique to Harlem and the New

York City area. Whenever I talk to people about it from other places, invariably they know nothing about it. People, more commonly, know of the basketball-related games called "horse" and "around the world," but five-two is not as well known.

Though not a game for working on one's dribbling, jumping, defense, stamina, or passing, it is indeed a way to work on one's shooting and trash talking (of which there was always plenty in games of five-two). Five-two was taken so seriously that people often played for money. By that time I was already too hooked on candy, soda, and the like to put what little bit of money I had up for grabs in games of five-two. So when it came to playing for money, I preferred sitting in the shade with a snack to watch the action from the sidelines.

When I did play, it was for the fun of playing, or for what we called "boonks-up." Boonks-up means what it sounds like. If you lost, you had to go under the basket and bend over with your backside towards the free-throw line. Then anyone who scored higher than the person who lost had several chances to get a running start to the free-throw line to throw the basketball at the loser's backside. If the targeted person did not keep an eye on the person throwing the ball, some kids liked to sneak up to get a good hard blast with the ball at close range.

Five-two is fun, easy, and can be played by just about anyone, and it is actually a good way to introduce kids to basketball. It takes 30, 52, or any predetermined number of points to win. Sometimes, to make the game more interesting, we played to 100 points or more. Each player takes turns shooting from the top of the circle that the foul line cuts in half, just inside the 3-point half circle (called the key). For kids that are too small to shoot from the key, this shot can be taken from the foul line or even closer. After the shot, the shooter should try to recover the ball as close to the basket as possible. This makes the second shot easier. If the ball goes out of bounds before the shooter gets it, the second shot has to be taken from the out-of-bounds line where the ball went out. If the ball goes out of bounds under the basket, the second shot needs to be taken from the free-throw line. The first shot is worth five points, and the second shot is worth two, hence the name, five-two. If the shooter's first shot misses everything, the second shot is forfeited, and it is the next person's turn.

On the other hand, a shooter who makes both shots gets to shoot again. So conceivably, if a good shooter got a hot hand, he or she could reel off a string of successful shot attempts until they win the game. We called this "running a game." This means someone can run their number of points up quickly to win the game without their opponents getting a chance to shoot again, or shoot at all sometimes if a particularly good shooter goes first. If it seems unfair to lose a game and perhaps one's money without getting a chance to shoot, this is not exactly true. What determines who takes the first shot is a series of shots before the game starts. So whoever continues to make their shots, when the others miss, gets to go first. So the shooting order is determined by who makes this series of shots. Hence, one's shooting ability is crucial, and the stakes were even higher when money was involved. A person's pockets could be emptied out or filled up at the end of a succession of five-two games.

Though my sweet-tooth cravings precluded me from putting my few dollars up for grabs, playing five-two (for money) for one of my friends was not a problem, at all. His name was William Hines, and he was the left fielder on our softball team. Playing softball, he caught just about anything hit near him. As young as he was, he played left field with the skill and flair of a professional baseball player. He covered left field tirelessly, and he had a rifle of an arm that regularly cut down any base runner that dared to put his accurate and powerful throwing arm to the test. Then when it came to basketball and five-two, he was just as good, if not better.

William was one of my best friends, and I say this proudly not only because of his intelligence and shooting ability, but most of all because of the exceptional person he has always been; Stephen Curry reminds me of William in a lot of ways. From early on, everyone knew how well he shot, but as his reputation continued to grow, he was soon known all over Harlem and NYC. Along with that, he was one of the most decent, dignified, respectful, inspiring, intelligent, humble, fun, and funny people I have ever met. He was a child prodigy and he spoke and carried himself with the confidence and distinction of a college professor at only 9 years old. So with his intelligence, dedication, size, discipline, and physicality, he pushed his shooting and other basketball skills to a level that no one from the neighborhood came close to replicating, and there were plenty of excellent basketball players in and around our neighborhood.

Because of his remarkable shooting touch, William deservedly earned the nickname "Shotgun" years later while in college. During his college home-game warm-ups, they played Junior Walker's hit tune, Shotgun, while William drained jump shots from all over the court. This warm-up/shooting exhibit, I am sure, had to be unsettling for their opposing teams, and even more so for the people who had to guard him. As kids, we called William "Crook-arm." This name came as a result of the rather odd and crooked way he held his free arm while he dribbled the ball and concentrated on getting into position to release his deadly shot. It seemed that there were not enough nicknames to capture such an interesting person. William used to encourage us all to read more. He told us that the more we read the better we would get at it. So at that age, not only was he intelligent, but he was thoughtful enough to share this valuable piece of advice with his friends. He continued by encouraging us to read everything from books, magazines, newspapers, comic books, and anything else we could get our hands on. Not only that, but he practiced what he preached; he always bought, read, or at least had a rolled up copy of the New York Daily News stuffed in his back pocket to read later.

Being the highly distinguished collection of knuckleheads that we were, we always looked for anything we could find to tease people about. But because there was so little to tease William about, the best we could do was harp on how much he practiced his shooting. Very often and early in the morning, I would hear someone bouncing a basketball on one of P.S. 125's basketball courts. Then, when I looked out the window to see who it was, more often than not, it would be William, by himself working on his shot, and sometimes it would be in midwinter with ice or snow on the ground. William didn't seem to mind the ribbing, and he actually laughed at it right along with everyone else. Without any of us knowing, he was already thinking two or three steps ahead of everyone, and he never gave us the slightest hint that he knew he would soon have the last laugh. Then before long, all of his practicing started to pay off, and everything changed; at that point, he was the only one laughing.

Suddenly and seemingly out of nowhere, and much like what we see Stephen Curry doing now, as he seems to make defenders spin in circles or disappear as they struggle to guard him, he started to make just about every shot he took. It's one thing to have a hot shooting hand from time to time, but with William it was another story altogether. Unlike the rest of us, he didn't have "on" and "off" days; his shooting hand was always hot, and his basketball playing was built on skill, determination, dedication, practice, and discipline. Even while warming up, he hardly missed. I don't remember him ever once having an off day, and I played basketball with him all the time. If you were on his team, all you had to do was get the ball to him and you would never lose. Then, for those on the opposing team, trying to stop him was impossible. Sometimes when he saw us stumbling around and tripping over our feet trying to guard him, he would take one quick step back and shoot. Then, if he felt particularly expansive at the time, as soon as the ball left his hands, he would laugh. He laughed because he knew that the ball was going to go in, and he knew that no one was going to be able to do anything about it. Then when everyone's eyes turned towards the basket, nine or (very often) ten times out of ten, it would result in another two points. We didn't have nets on our playground baskets, so instead of hearing the splash of a net, there would be silence, and then the sound of the ball bouncing after it passed through the (orange-colored, cast-iron, heavy-duty, NYC playground) hoop, at dead center.

Armed with this deadly shot, William was a force to be reckoned with when it came to five-two, and he was happy to take anyone on who wanted to put their shooting touch or money to the test. He was so good that he played five-two with the older guys. One person that he played with a lot was a guy that everyone called Stamp. Stamp used to come to our neighborhood and schoolyard for the sole purpose of playing five-two with William. They would go at it for hours on end, while trash talking each other at every step of the way. My friends and I used to sit on the sidelines, watching in amazement, as William enthusiastically drained one shot after the other with the end of a lollipop stick hanging from the side of his mouth, while taunting Stamp relentlessly.

Stamp was an interesting guy and a very good shooter too. He was older than us, and known as being a pretty tough character throughout the neighborhood. I never knew why he was called Stamp, but it was likely for a very good reason. Single handedly he could have stamped or pounded all of us into the ground and taken all of our money if he wanted to, but he never did anything like that. He never played in any of the pickup games, and he was always well dressed. It seemed that getting his fine clothes soiled and sweaty by playing pickup games was beneath him, so playing five-two for money was his specialty. It was clear that he respected William for both his intelligence and his shooting touch, but most of all he seemed to appreciate William's competitive spirit. After all, William was the only youngster who was bold enough to take him on in games of five-two for money. So when William won, Stamp would just fork over the cash and then looked forward to trying to win it back in the next game.

Being the pure shooter and skillful ballplayer William had become, he could have become a professional basketball player in the NBA. I do not know why this never happened, but any NBA team would have been better with such a talented and intelligent ballplayer in their lineup. He was a phenomenon in so many ways, and he made our junior high and high school teams with ease. Seeing him in the neighborhood many years later, he told me that he'd been offered 37 college scholarships, and chose to study and play basketball at North Carolina A&T. William also played with such notables as Nate "Tiny" Archibald, Charlie Scott, Kareem Abdul-Jabbar, and Earl "The Pearl" Monroe. He told me that in one shooting exhibit he made 83 shots consecutively from two feet behind the key. Among William's other accomplishments, he wrote three books about Harlem basketball: "The Harlem Basketball Hall of Fame – 1958-1980," "Living to Tell the Tale," and his third book is called "The History of Harlem Basketball the Evolution." William "Shotgun" Hines was always a class act, and a true friend. Those who have had the pleasure of knowing him will say the same thing. There will be more to say about William since our friendship went well beyond the parameters of basketball. Over the years, William, Steven Wright, Charlie Valdez, Kenneth Miller, and me were an inseparable quintet of friends. We went to house parties, Latin dances, played basketball, rode the subway trains, and hung out all over Harlem, Greenwich Village, the Bronx, and Manhattan, laughing, joking, and having loads of fun.

With my summer work assignment completed, much to my relief, I was able to move on to the sixth grade with the rest of my classmates. My sixth grade teacher's name was Mr. Kamermeyer, and from the first day it was clear that he was one of those special teachers that kids adore. Somehow he was able to harness our restless energy, channel it into learning, and get the best from all of us. With his patience, presence, easygoing personality, and excellent teaching style, we all knew that he had our best interest at heart. As a result, classroom clowning was not an issue for him at all, and he had one hundred percent class participation all the time. There were never any detentions, ear pulling, or bathroom invasions with him. Not only that, but never once did Mr. Kamermeyer ever have to raise his voice to discipline anyone. Be it science, math, social studies, or reading, Mr. Kamermeyer had a way of making it all fun and interesting, while making us all feel very good about studying hard and learning. My mother was amazed by this sustained change in my heightened level of productivity and attitude about school. Though she never met him, she'd certainly heard enough about him from me, and she saw the positive impact he was having on me too.

Midway through the school year and catching us by surprise, Mr. Kamermeyer announced that in two weeks, he would be leaving P.S. 125 and transferring out to teach at another school. We were all stunned into silence, and I remember being hit particularly hard by the news. Right when I was finally starting to find my footing and reap the rewards of this more dedicated and disciplined approach to schoolwork, the one teacher who made it happen would soon be gone. Being the excellent teacher that he was, some principal must have heard about him and decided to pluck him up and right out of our midst. In the end, we had no choice but to accept this bitter reality and enjoy the last two weeks we had with him.

On Mr. Kamermeyer's last day, I was the last one to see him before he left the building. At the end of the day, I was coming up the staircase, as he was on his way down and out of the building for the last time. He stopped, shook my hand, and gave me his best wishes. He told me that I was a good kid, and he encouraged me to work hard. Then he told me that he knew that I would be able to do or get whatever I wanted out of life. Then he was gone, down the stairs, and out of the building. I'd never had a teacher say anything so encouraging to me before, and I never forgot it.

Then too, to this day, I still very much remember and appreciate his very kind and supportive words.

Our new teacher came in to replace him that following Monday. His name was Mr. Rush. Mr. Rush was a good teacher too. But having to fill Mr. Kamermeyer's shoes would have been a tall order for anyone. As a result it was not long before some of the loose cannons became unhinged, and the classroom clowning started to pick up again.

Nevertheless, because of my short but productive time with Mr. Kamermeyer, his supportive words to me, and coming ever so close to having to repeat the fifth grade, it all helped to kept me on the straight and narrow for the rest of the year. So I had a decent final year at P.S. 125 before moving on to junior high school.

Despite my academic struggles, my elementary school experience was not bad. I attended two good schools, had dedicated teachers, and was given a reasonably good educational foundation. Another good thing that came with going to school in New York City was the seemingly limitless opportunities for interesting fieldtrips. The fieldtrips were what I enjoyed most of all. Before my six years of elementary school were completed, I'd been to the Bronx Zoo, the Museum of Natural History, the Brooklyn Botanical Gardens, the Hayden Planetarium, Central Park, the Central Park Zoo, the Empire State Building, Chinatown, and to the Statue of Liberty.

On the hot spring day that we took the South Ferry to the Statue of Liberty, it was the first time I'd ridden on a boat of any kind; and I remember thinking that the boat was going to sink as I stepped onboard. Clearly, we made it to Liberty Island and back, safely. While at Liberty Island we took the elevator up to the top of the base of the statue, and climbed the long spiral stairs up to the crown. Then from the small windows in the crown, we had a spectacular view of Manhattan and its harbor from this unique and picturesque vantage point, and gracious gift to the United States by France after World War II (a classy diplomatic gesture that countries do not do for each other anymore these days, unfortunately, but need to start doing again, and right away).

Being free from any assignments to keep me from having to repeat the sixth grade, there was plenty of time for me to play baseball, basketball, and enjoy my summer vacation. With my friends in tow, my father took us everywhere. If we were not going to Coney Island's amusement park, we went to Pelham Bay Park, Central Park, Van Cortland Park, Crotona Park, or High Bridge Pool to swim, picnic, or to just throw, catch, and hit a baseball around. This was what my new neighborhood had to offer, and it provided me with good times in just about every way. Given all that it had to offer, and given all that I saw and learned during my relatively short time living there, it made 12 years seem more like 30.

3

A New Neighborhood with Everything a Kid Like Me Could Have Wanted

We were all very excited about moving on to junior high school. Being the crowning achievement that it was for us, it as well extended the boundaries of our neighborhood outward even more. This made it possible for us to meet and learn about the people in this unexplored section of the general area. There were more tenement apartment buildings and another large housing unit called Manhattanville near the school. Manhattanville has as many people as Grant, and their buildings are just as tall. So with J.H.S. 43 accepting students from Grant, Manhattanville, and all of the other neighboring communities, we had students coming and going in all directions.

The one thing that concerned us had to do with something called rookie-ing. It was an initiation of sorts that first year students were said to have to undergo. We heard about rookie-ing during our last year of elementary school, and it was the one cloud hanging over our heads that tainted the thrill of starting this next phase of our education. As we'd heard, new male students would be forced to carry the books of the eighth and ninth graders at the end of the first day. Word had it, too, that if someone refused, there would be consequences from the older students.

I was sure that there was going to be trouble. I knew that I wasn't going to carry anyone's books, and I was sure that someone would take exception to my defiance. Making matters worse was the fact that I didn't see a teacher or school staff anywhere nearby who could have prevented something like this from happening. When I reached the corner of the block, I saw a group of older guys standing around, but not as much as a single one of them paid the slightest bit of attention to me. Then, as I continued on my way, much to my relief, I realized that this whole book-carrying initiation was nothing more than someone's idea of how to stir up some anxiety for us seventh graders.

Unlike elementary school, where we were assigned to one classroom and one teacher, in junior high school we changed classrooms, subjects, and teachers every hour. There were eight periods of classes, and it greatly alleviated the boredom and difficulty of sitting in one classroom all day. It seemed to make the school day go by a lot faster too.

The importance given to clothes and dressing was something else that was different about going to junior high school. Being kids living in one of the fashion capitals of the world, this attention that we gave to clothing had worked its way right into our poor and working-class communities. "Being clean" was a short and sweet two-worded phrase that we all knew and used to capture our passion for dressing well. The dress code was strictly adhered to, right down to the type of sneakers we wore. So if someone were not wearing Converse All Stars, Pro-Keds, or (what we called) track shoes, they could have expected to hear about it from someone, or, at least, get a quick sideways glance down at their feet every now and then. So everyone had a clear sense of what passed muster and what didn't, when it came to " being clean." Unfortunately, for far too many, this focus on clothing seemed to have gotten more of our attention than our studies. This was a fact that was both sad and true, so attending "43" was like being at a fashion show.

Unlike the sagging pants, sideways caps, hoodies, grills, and extra-large T-shirts that we see today, we dressed in a style we called Ivy League. To me, the two words meant nothing more than a style of dress that made certain items of clothing a must. Other than that, I was clueless about the meaning of the two words. So with our cuffed pants, patched-pocket blazers, All-American brand sweaters, Duffer brand overcoats, buttoned-down collars, penny loafers, wingtip Quartervans, Playboys or Desert Boots on our feet, and broad, striped neckties, we were clones of each other (much like the kids today) when it came to dressing. But no one could tell us a thing; as far as we were concerned, we were just a little bit too cool for school, as the saying goes. Though we dressed like the college students at Columbia University and the City College of New York, academics and the like did not top our lists of priorities, unfortunately.

Adding to that problem, there was a double standard that divided us into two general categories when it came to the types of classes we were allowed to take. Students who excelled academically were provided one course curriculum, while the others were placed in another group of classes. Due to problems with behavior, learning, or a decision made by school officials, this second group was placed in classes that were modified, watered down, and not very stimulating in an intellectual sense; something that is now more widely known, and is called tracking. Though it doesn't seem practical to mix high and low achievers together in the same classes, this arrangement did cause kids like me to fall through the cracks of our educational system. In spite of my problems, it might have been good to mix me in with the high achievers. The chances were good that I might have been inspired by the more stimulating subjects, environment, and the academically inclined students (not to mention, perhaps, the better teachers). As I maintain, my problems were related to learning and had nothing to do with behavior. I wanted to do better, but I continued to struggle. Many of us were placed in classes that appeared to be designed for little more than fulfilling the requirement of attending school. This left us with little to show for it at the end of the line. The reality was that our school was only a part of a much larger educational system that was like a conveyor belt that ensured there would be room for the next group of seventh graders coming in. So if someone did not have access to these more substantive classes, they were just out of luck. Hence, this diluted education took a lot away from many of us at a very important time in our lives.

I'd been concerned about this two-tier educational system for some time, but it bothered me even more at the junior high school level. I didn't like it and was even embarrassed by being forced to take these substandard classes. Although we all carried a full load of classes, our course curriculum was a scholastic wasteland in many ways. Then too, given our inability to see or understand our plight (not to mention our almost single-minded focus on clothes and fashion), unwittingly, we were accomplices in our own educational shortfall.

This is a problem that does not seem to get better. Now, as an adult, I see so many inner-city kids who are much more enthusiastic about standing around outside their school buildings, rather than spending that time in their classrooms or in the library. With public schools closing, losing funding, and teachers getting so little support, combined with this pervasive low regard for education, it all makes for a true recipe for disaster.

I could have benefited so much if my school had provided me with just a little bit more. But my efforts to get an upgrade in my classes were repeatedly denied because it was felt that I would have not been able to handle the more challenging workload; and quite possibly they could have been right. I cannot deny that I played a big part in creating the problems I was having. As bad as my focus was, I was not a completely hopeless case; I knew the importance of a good education. If I had been given a little more to work with, it might have been just enough to give me the spark I needed to get me engaged and moving in the right direction (as it happened for me in Mr. Kamermeyer's class). So I think the school dropped the ball, too, by denying me a chance at these better classes, or for not trying to work them into my studies, gradually, to see how I would have done with them. With that being the case, and from the school system's perspective, they had the task of bringing kids in and shipping kids out.

Despite my diluted classes and academic struggles, attending J.H.S. 43 was not a complete waste of three years. We were all energetic and bright in our own ways, and there were other classes that kept us reasonably engaged. Our physically unfit gym teacher sat high atop a wooden platform with a whistle around his neck. From his lofty perch, he sipped tea and munched on crackers while he, audibly, led us through a series of stretches, deep-knee bends, crunches, pushups, toe touches, and other types of calisthenics. He laughed and commented when he heard our knees cracking and popping while we did our deep-knee bends. After that, he would organize us into dodge ball teams by class and entertained himself by eating and watching us try to knock the stuffing out of each other with the dodge balls. Basketball was also a part of our physical education program too.

We were taught to type and our typing classroom had one manual typewriter bolted down to each desk. There were no letters on the keys, so this prevented us from forming the habit of looking down to find the keys. As a guide there was a chart at the front of the classroom with a layout of the keys and their corresponding letters. So by looking at only the chart and our exercise books (with our fingers on the rest keys), we practiced our typing drills for an hour every day. The, 40 or so, typewriters clicked and clacked like a slow, a-rhythmic percussion symphony, and I will never forget the sound. First with the right hand, as slow as molasses and completely out of sync: juj (space) kik (space) lol (space) ;p; (space) and then the left hand: frf (space) ded (space) sws (space) aqa (space). As a result, I am a pretty good typist now, and I use my fingers correctly.

We had classes in math, history, biology, social studies, and English, but mine, as I mentioned, were of a watered-down variety. A class that did have a profound and lasting impact on me was one on drug abuse. We learned about how people became addicted to hard drugs after only a few casual or experimental uses. I knew nothing about drugs prior to this. So it was very sobering for me to learn the hard and cold facts about drug abuse. The girls were given classes called home economics. It sounds fancy, but for the most part, it was for nothing more than preparing them to be housewives. There was another class we were given called merchandising. It sounds fancy too, but it essentially taught us how to be store clerks. These merchandising and home economics classes were at the bottom rung of our school's course curriculum.

We did, however, have Spanish classes. Given the Spanish that I already knew and the promise I made to myself to learn it to the best of my ability, these classes were enjoyable for me, and I did well with them. Though both Spanish and French were taught at "43," because of an unspoken, illusory, but prevailing notion that French was the more sophisticated of the two, it was only offered to the advanced students. So without me having a say in the matter, Spanish was the language that was chosen for me. But much like my typing classes, this worked in my favor. Not only did studying Spanish help me to fulfill the biggest promise I made to myself, but there was no one in the neighborhood who I could have spoken French with. So studying Spanish was perfect for me.

My homeroom teacher, Mrs. Tate, was my Spanish teacher, and she was a serious person who hardly ever smiled. But she was a very good Spanish teacher who spoke with a very good Spanish accent. During our first day in her class, I remember her teaching us how to say, "I am from Chile." She said it several times with a very serious facial expression, and she asked us to repeat it until we got it right: "Soy de Chile, soy de Chile."

Seated next to me in Mrs. Tate's class was a bright and confident kid named Carlton. He was light years ahead of us and even light years ahead of the high achievers in the advanced classes, for that matter. Given his maturity and intelligence, had he been given a chance with the advanced classes, the sky could have been the limit for him. I imagine that someone calling the shots did not care much for Carlton's precociousness. So perhaps in an effort to contain him, or to knock him down a peg or two, he was placed on the marginal side of our educational divide.

Deservedly so, Carlton was voted the most popular male student in our class. Then too, in keeping with 43's trademark of high fashion, he was always well dressed; he wore a wide assortment of professionally laundered shirts, colorful neckties, and sharp sport jackets. Additionally, when he wanted to, Carlton was quite capable of stirring things up in a classroom. Putting his active mind to work, he could come up with some pretty interesting ways to throw a wrench into the proceedings, and exasperate a teacher to no end. He didn't do it much, and he was not disruptive, generally speaking. Actually, he was pretty well behaved, and he seemed to be from good parents and a good family; but if something bothered him, he did not hesitate letting it be known in one way or another. One case in point had to do with what he did in our English class one day.

Our English teacher's name was Mrs. Tingling and she looked like what you might expect an old school, strict English teacher named Mrs. Tingling to look like. She was an African-American woman, and she wore her hair rolled into a tight bun at the back of her head without a single strand of hair out of place. Very prim, proper, and smug, she wore a permanent scowl on her face; it appeared as if she had a bad taste in her mouth that wouldn't go away. So, like Mrs. Tate, humor and warmth were neither of her dominant personality traits, and it was clear that she didn't seem to care all that much for us. Carlton knew it, and he didn't care much for her either. Aloof, distant, prudish, humorless, and disdainful, Mrs. Tingling made Mrs. Tate's class seem lighthearted and cheerful by comparison. Mrs. Tate came close to smiling every now and then, but Mrs. Tingling's sour expression never changed.

Not at all appreciative of her attitude towards us, Carlton decided to show his displeasure while a silent reading assignment was underway. He started to hum the song "She'll Be Coming Around the Mountain When She Comes." His song selection, alone, was funny in and unto itself; and he very likely chose it to add some humor to his protest, for us. Apparently, detecting the source of the humming was not easy given the size of our classroom and the way sound carried. Mrs. Tingling did her best to spot the culprit by scanning the classroom carefully while we each peeked up to see her reaction to it. Further complicating matters for her was the fact that there were two or three others who, too, could have been responsible for the errant behavior.

With her thumb and hawkish eyes weighing in on us heavily, we could see that she was not happy about it at all, but she seemed to be unable to pinpoint where it was coming from. Eventually, she announced to everyone that humming was not allowed in her classroom. Carlton stopped, momentarily, and soon started to hum again. Becoming increasingly angry, I saw her eyes dart around the room in vain as she tried her best to spot the defiant student. Carlton's humming continued intermittently until Mrs. Tingling started to ask people individually. So in a stern but muted voice that barely contained her anger, she asked, and each student responded, "Tyrone, is that you humming?" "No, Mrs. Tingling." "Charles, is that you?" "No, Mrs. Tingling." Then when she got to Carlton, this was when everything hit the fan. Indignant, and like an impassioned attorney, Carlton tore into Mrs. Tingling by arguing his innocence and challenging her for accusing him in a way that none of us would have ever done. His defensive stance was such that it rocked the, always, staid and stoic Mrs. Tingling back on her heels. So with no hard and clear evidence, she did not up the ante by arguing back at him or tossing him out of the classroom for speaking to her in the way that he did. Then perhaps satisfied that he had successfully tweaked her nose in front of everyone, like a trained actor, he quickly regained his composure and turned his attention back to his assignment as if it all had never happened.

At report card time Mrs. Tate wrote a note in the teacher's comment section of my report card about the influence she thought Carlton was having on me, and how much it concerned her. While I watched my mother read my report card (shaking her head) I felt a sickening feeling in the pit of my stomach. After reading it, she asked me why my grades were not better. Then she wanted to know who Carlton is, and she wanted to know why did he have so much of an influence on me. So before I knew it, I was back in the same old rut again with my grades and schoolwork. My mother was upset, and I was disappointed knowing that my grades were not better. So now it was going to be up to me to try to rally whatever I had to get a better handle on my faltering study habits. This, as I knew, would not only be for my own good, but as well so that I would not cause so much grief and anguish for my mother.

If that were not enough, one great difficulty my family and I faced during that time was my father's illness and passing. Before matters became very serious, there were two or three times he was admitted to the hospital for long periods of time. Then one day my mother's brother broke the news to my siblings and me. I was thirteen years old at the time, and after telling us, he took me to the side and told me that it was going to be my responsibility to help my mother by looking out for the family and household since I was the oldest male.

My father's funeral service was held at a popular church in the neighborhood called Church of the Master. The influential pastor Rev. Eugene Calendar conducted the service. The large turnout from the neighborhood spoke to the person my father was, and what he meant to us and to so many people from the neighborhood. He was given full military honors, and three soldiers shot rifles and a bugler played Taps. Another soldier folded a flag into a triangle, and handed it to my mother. Then after taking it, she broke down in tears clutching the folded flag.

My father was pretty special; he was unique, interesting, insightful, and funny too when he wanted to be. Domestic strife, violence, drinking, and shouting were not parts of who he was as a person; I never once heard him raise his voice. He worked hard and gave us a very good life and childhood. Since we'd lost so many years with him, I often think of what it would have been like to have him with us longer. Sometimes I wonder what it would be like to talk to him now as an adult and delve more into his innermost thoughts and life experiences. He was very dignified; and, by losing him while we were so young, there is so much about him that I never got to know.

Not long after this profound family tragedy, a Japanese friend who lived nearby told me about a Boy Scout troop he belonged to, and he asked me to come to one of the scout meetings. His name is Paul Kimizuka, and he lived a block away, on Amsterdam Avenue. I was well aware of the Boy Scout organization, but it never occurred to me to join. But Paul spoke so enthusiastically about Troop 557 that he easily convinced me to go. On my first night, we took a bus to a church on the corner of 86th Street and Amsterdam Avenue. The meetings were held in the gym of the West Park Presbyterian Church that was built in 1892. I had so much fun at my first meeting that I decided to join long before it was time to go home. The troop was made up of Japanese, Puerto Rican, Irish, Jewish, Italian, and African-American kids, so we were a real mixed bag of a scout troop. Our meetings were held upstairs in the church's gymnasium, and the spacious gym gave us plenty of room for our three scout patrols, our meetings, and other scouting activities.

Being the unwavering source of support my mother has always been for me, she gave me money for a uniform as soon as I asked. So, with my new uniform, I felt even more a part of Troop 557. At the end of each meeting, one person was chosen to be the outstanding scout for the night.

Our uniforms were inspected, so we prepared by ironing our shirts, pants, hats and scarves, shining our shoes, and polishing our belt buckles. After several attempts, I was finally chosen. I soon convinced several friends of mine to come, and they joined too. So on Friday evenings, we met in front of my building, and took the bus to the West Park Presbyterian Church for a fun-filled night of scouting activities.

After our meetings, we played basketball in the gym before going home. Before calling it a night, we stopped at "Maria's" for a slice of pizza and a soda. Hands down, Maria had the best pizza I have ever tasted. With perfect crust, her special blend of tomato sauce, seasoning, and cheese, it was a very good deal having such good and piping hot pizza for 15 cents a slice, and 10 cents for a cup of soda. Given Maria's limited English and old-country persona, her fine pizza recipe could have been from right out of Italy.

To move through the scout's ranking system, we studied and were tested on what we learned from our scouting manuals. Reading maps, using a compass, tying knots, chopping wood, pitching tents, applying first aid, building fires, and learning the Morse Code were only some of our activities. As we studied and fulfilled our various scouting requirements for merit badges, we advanced in rank and went from Tenderfoot, Third, Second, and then First-class scout. Then our studies became more advanced, and we could go on from First-class scout to Star, Life, and then Eagle Scout.

Because Troop 557 was comprised largely of Japanese scouts, we had access to judo classes once a week. Then, too, on camping trips, we ate Japanese food long before it became the popular fare that it is now. The best thing about our scout troop was that we regularly left the city for overnight camping trips. Not only did this give us a chance to get out of the city, but we were able to try our hands at many of the things we learned from our scouting handbooks. So we packed our army-surplus backpacks, with food, tents, sleeping bags, axes, hatchets, first aid kits, scout knives, water buckets, canteens, clothes, pots, pans, and other camping gear. Then we would take off to spend the weekend in the wilderness, roughing it by sleeping in tents, sleeping bags, and under the trees, stars, moon, and open sky.

Our favorite place for camping was the Harriman State Park in Sloatsburg, N.Y. It is one of the largest parks in New York State. It is a massive 46,613-acre park with 200 miles of hiking trails, 31 lakes, and streams of fresh, clean, and crystal clear water. Fathers of scouts with cars took us up to Rockland County in a long car caravan. After dropping us off, without the conveniences of city life, a cabin, or a camper to retreat to when the sun and the temperature went down at night, we were out and on our own. This was very new and different for a gaggle of city boys like us. Our scoutmaster was a real adventurer, because once a camping date was set, we always followed through with it, rain or snow notwithstanding. After unloading our gear from the cars, we would start our long hike into the woods to find our campsite. With our heavy steel-framed backpacks digging into our backs, and our flashlights lighting the way, we hiked for 40 minutes to an hour along narrow trails, over hills, and along streams of water to our destination. Then in the dead of night, with our flashlights and lanterns, we pitched our tents, unrolled our sleeping bags, and emptied our backpacks to turn in for the night.

In the morning, we filled our water buckets, gathered leaves, twigs, rocks, and firewood. Then we built campfires to offset the early morning chill and cook our breakfasts. Though we had something called Halazone tablets to purify any water that may have not been safe to drink, we never had to use them. The water was always potable, clean, and fresh. So we had all the water we needed from fresh streams that were only a few yards away from our favorite campsite areas. I might add that it was some of the coldest and most refreshing water I have ever quenched my thirst with, and I hope that it is still as fresh and clean now as it was then.

After breakfast we would spend the day reading, studying, chopping wood, and practicing the things we would be tested on. We learned how to identify plants that were both helpful and harmful. We also learned to identify broken bones, abrasions, bruises, snakebite, burns, poison ivy, heat stroke, lacerations, and shock while learning about the types of first aid needed for each of these conditions and situations. After studying and taking our various tests, we would spend the rest of the day climbing trees, hiking, exploring, and learning about the natural surroundings that were so much unlike the large city where we spent so much of our time. After lunch we would spend the rest of the day playing games, relaxing, or studying before having dinner. At the Saturday night campfire gatherings, our scoutmaster told stories, we sang songs, and toasted marshmallows before going to sleep.

But before calling it a night, all new scouts needed to be initiated into something called "the fly family." During the time leading up to everyone's first camping trip, new scouts were told vague but scary stories about these initiations, but no one would ever be specific or divulge a full and clear picture of what it involved. Based on what we were told, each scout had to be initiated, and it didn't sound like fun. There were stories as outrageous as scouts being burned with hot embers, to having hot splinters of wood shoved under their fingernails. With this composite of vague and jumbled stories, we were told that if a scout were not able to endure the painful ordeal, he would be excluded from many scouting activities until his initiation was completed.

On my first camping trip there were six of us scheduled to meet the fly family. After hearing these chilling stories, we were all very concerned. Once the campfire fun, singing, storytelling, and games were over, the scoutmaster snapped us back to reality by announcing that it was time to initiate the new scouts into the fly family. Instantly, the bottom dropped right out of all the fun I'd been having up to that point. Now with all hope gone that the fly family talk was just another hoax or that the initiation had slipped the scoutmasters mind, I knew that my time had come. The scoutmaster asked the new scouts to stand and follow one of the senior scouts into the woods. There, we had to stand and wait for ten agonizing minutes while things were prepared for our initiation. Then with the beam of the senior scout's flashlight lighting the way, we each had to walk back to the campsite to be initiated, one at a time.

The first petrified scout followed the beam of light while we watched nervously and waited for our turns; I was the fourth one in line. After five minutes, we heard loud screams coming from the first scout being initiated. Then in succession, the second and the third scouts went for their turns. The same scenario played itself out each time with the screaming carrying through the woods and the, otherwise, quiet night, rattling my nerves even more.

When it was my turn, I followed the beam of light through the trees back to the campsite. There, I found everyone seated around the orange glow of what remained of our once robust campfire. Their heads were down, and there were six other scouts standing side by side with their heads down too. They had scarves covering their noses and mouths, so I was unable to see who was who. Their hands were behind their backs, and by bending their knees slightly, they bounced up and down while making a buzzing noise that mimicked the sound of buzzing flies. I looked around to see if I could spot the three scouts who had been initiated before me, but I didn't see them. Then I thought to myself that they were likely in one of the tents having their cuts and wounds treated; and I shuddered at the thought of joining them shortly.

The scoutmaster spoke to me in the same somber tone he ended the campfire gathering with. "Well Burrell, as you know, this is your initiation into the fly family." He spoke slowly dragging out each word, intentionally, to prolong the suspense and agony. When he asked me if I had any questions, I quickly told him, "No." I wanted him to hurry things along to get it over with and done as soon as possible. Next, he took me over to the six scouts standing side by side. They continued staring at the ground and continued buzzing menacingly for the entire time. The scoutmaster started by introducing me to Mr. Housefly. Then with what sounded like a mischievous dare, he asked me to shake hands with Mr. Housefly. Slowly and cautiously I put my hand out to shake hands with Mr. Housefly, and I got no response from him at all. He ignored me, and buzzed more agitatedly with his hands still behind his back. After ten seconds or so, and right when I started to withdraw my hand, Mr. Housefly started to buzz even louder, and then he quickly shot his hand out to shake my hand. It felt as if my heart had skipped three beats. I shook hands with Mr. Housefly, and the scoutmaster moved me along to the next one in line.

The introductions continued with each name changing. So I met Mr. Housefly, Mr. Horsefly, Mr. Shoofly, Mr. Fruit fly, Mr. Tsetse fly and so on until we reached the last one in line. Then the scoutmaster said to me, "Now I want you to shake hands with Mr. Dragonfly." I put my hand out, waited, and got no response from Mr. Dragonfly, as he continued to buzz and bounce up and down with all of the others. The constant buzzing added to my anxiety, and kept me on edge the entire time. With a name like Mr. Dragonfly and because he was the last one, I expected everything to hit the fan at that point. With bated breath I held my hand out, waited, and got no response from Mr. Dragonfly at all. Then when I started to withdraw my hand, Mr. Dragonfly pulled a wet towel out from behind his back and swatted me on the top of my head with it. I thought that this was the flashpoint, and I braced myself for whatever was to come next. Then I heard two or three scouts start to laugh, and at that point, I realized that it was all another harmless hoax. The scoutmaster quickly urged everyone to quiet down since there were two more scouts that needed to be initiated. After that, he told me to scream to further frighten the remaining two scouts. So I screamed, and was given the towel and a scarf to cover my nose and mouth with, and was told to take Mr. Dragonfly's place in the lineup. Then I was told to whack the next scout over the head with it when he puts his hand out to shake my hand; and the next scout was sent. After the last scout was hit with the towel, we added more wood to the campfire and gathered around the growing flames to talk and laugh about the funny things each terrified scout did. We also heard about and laughed at the outrageous fly family stories from the past. As we were told, during past fly family initiations, some scouts were so afraid that they took off running even deeper into the woods, and they had to be searched for, found, and brought back.

In the end, I was relieved to know that being smacked on the head with a wet towel and having my nerves rattled were going to be the extent of my fly family torture. We then added wood to the campfire, sang more songs, and, eventually, went to sleep for the night, very much looking forward to the time when we would be able to scare the daylights out of the next group of scouts who would go through the same unnerving ordeal.

After another night's sleep we would have breakfast, spend our last few hours enjoying the great outdoors, packing up, extinguishing the campfire, cleaning the campsite, and hiking back out to the road from where the cars took us back to the city.

Seeing how much I enjoyed these camping trips, my mother paid to send me to the Ten Mile River Scout Camp one summer. The TMR Scout

Camp is in Narrowsburg, N.Y. and is roughly an hour and a half outside of Manhattan. TMR is 12,000-acres, and camping there was not as raw as camping at Harriman State Park. TMR was exclusively and specifically designed for scouting activities. Instead of sleeping on the ground and in tents, we slept on cots and in cabin-like structures called lean-tos. Scouts came to TMR from all over New York State and New Jersey. We worked, studied, and played together for our two-week stay. There were large inter-troop campfire gatherings, we swam, rowed boats, and did skeet shooting. I didn't realize how much I enjoyed myself until I got back to Manhattan. After our usual weekend camping trips, I was always more than happy to get back to city life again. But after two weeks in the beauty, green, tranquility, fresh air, and natural surroundings of TMR, when I saw the cars, rooftops, concrete, and brick buildings again, all I wanted to do was turn around to go back up to the country. My less than enthusiastic reaction to the hustle and bustle of city life even surprised me.

Another scouting activity I was a part of was something called the Order of the Arrow. One scout from each troop was selected to spend a weekend working together. It was a disciplinary drill in that we had to work very hard, and we were not allowed to talk while we cleared fields, chopped wood, dug trenches, and ate our meals. After putting in a day-and-a half of work, I came close to ruining everything. Accidentally, I blurted out the first two or three words of a question and quickly stopped when I saw the look of shock and horror on someone's face. I became concerned, and thought that I would not pass. But I was given a break, and we all received our awards for completing our Order of the Arrow requirements. During our award ceremony and lunch, we were finally allowed to talk, socialize, and get to know each other. Then we were called up, and given pins and patches for our uniforms.

Getting a bicycle as a Christmas present was a nice surprise for me during my junior high school years. It was a beautiful red Schwinn, ten-speed racing bicycle that I was crazy about. After my friends and I had gotten our fill of riding around in the neighborhood, we set out to explore

Manhattan in a way that would have not been possible on foot or by public transportation. We rode practically everywhere and discovered so many of the city's interesting nooks and crannies. At the height of our bicycle craze, we used to ride from our building to Inwood Hill Park at the very northern end of Manhattan. Then we would turn around, ride back, pass through our neighborhood, and continue on to Battery Park at the southern end of the island. On much less ambitious outings, we used to ride to Central Park to explore the phenomenal green city in the middle of Manhattan. While there, we tried to cover as much of its 843 acres as possible before going home.

In our efforts to cover as much of Manhattan's 23.7 square miles as possible, more remarkable than the distance we rode was how we weaved in and out of New York City traffic without having one serious accident to speak of. Given our risky riding, it seemed as if a protective shield were around us at all times; there was not one single broken bone, cut, scrape, or bruise. Some of my friends actually rode hands free in the middle of traffic, and I even tried it a few times. We did it, not only to show and test our riding skills, but mostly to change the slumped over position that so much riding subjected us too. Now, riding a bicycle without holding on to the handlebars is something that I would not even think of doing again.

One time while riding very fast downhill on Amsterdam Avenue, I came dangerously close to doing an ignominious face plant on the sidewalk right in front of my building for everyone to see. Being the bicycle-riding novice I was at the time, I had never used my front breaks; so curiously and mistakenly, I chose that time to give it a try to see what would happen. Moving as fast as I was, in a downhill direction, I had no idea of the surprise that was in store for me. The front wheel came to a dead stop, and the rest of the bike continued forward. Then from the rear, my bicycle rose up and hurled me off the seat, and into the air. Before I knew it, I was on the ground, and my bicycle was about six feet away from me with the back wheel still spinning. Miraculously, the bicycle did not get a scratch, and I was not hurt at all. It startled me, but in the process I did experience Sir Isaac Newton's first law of motion, personally: An object in motion tends to stay in motion.

Another time while riding on the double yellow line that divided the fast moving, two way, busy, taxi filled, Midtown traffic, I saw another cyclist headed towards me. He was on the same yellow line, and slightly less than a block away. We were moving pretty fast, and we had very little wiggle room at our sides to pass each other easily. It did appear that we had enough time to coordinate a safe and easy way to get by each other, but our evasive actions mirrored each other in an unusually uncanny way. When I moved slightly to the right of the yellow line, he moved to his left. This kept us headed right towards each other. Then when I moved to my left, our evasive actions mirrored each other's again as he moved to his right. With cars shooting by us on both sides, I tried one more time to inch to my right; and when I did, I saw him go to his left again at the exact same time. At this point, we were getting pretty close to each other, and we had precious little time to get out of each other's way. I decided to stay on the yellow line to let him choose the side to pass me on this time. Then I saw that we had the same idea again. So now we were still headed towards each other, at a pretty lively clip, and on the verge of possibly the worst bicycle smashup of the year, without helmets, and in heavy, wild, fast moving, busy, Midtown Manhattan traffic. Oddly enough, it never occurred to either of us to squeeze our breaks to stop. With no time left for me to do anything, I stayed on the yellow line, lifted my feet off the pedals, drew my body up into a ball as much as possible, closed my eyes, and braced myself for the colossal hit. At the point of impact, I continued to wait, wait, and wait some more; and nothing happened. Then when I opened my eyes, I didn't see the guy in front of me anymore. It was as if he had disappeared into thin air. When I turned around to look behind me, I saw him on the same yellow line peddling south as I continued north. It seemed as if we had passed right through each other in some kind of inexplicable way. Though I didn't see what happened, clearly, he came up with a last second maneuver to avoid hitting me by what had to be fractions of an inch.

Not long after this close call, a new girl moved to the neighborhood and into my building. Given the excitement her sudden arrival stirred, having an ugly gash, scar, or dent in my forehead from a bicycle accident would have been untimely for me. We guys were all swooning and woozy after hearing the news. With our neighborhood's crackling hot grapevine being what it was, the news of her arrival threw us guys into a shark like frenzy before we had even seen her. Then when we did see her, it was unanimous; she lived right up to all the hype. We were all on our best Ps & Qs, and we made every effort to put our best foot forward. Her mother could have easily become annoyed as much as we appeared at their door with any kind of flimsy excuse to get in to see her daughter. Thinking that we were pulling the wool over her mother's eyes, we would always ask for her younger brother at the door. Fortunately for us, they were very nice people, and their mother was like an angel. She always welcomed us in with her beautiful smile, and she always treated us very well. Seeing the way that we practically tripped and stumbled over each other in our efforts to get her daughter's attention, she could barely contain her smile and laughter watching us love-struck knuckleheads carrying on in the shameless ways that we did.

Soon after, I heard that I had a slight edge over my smitten friends. Hearing the news made me feel good; I was close to having my first girlfriend. Finding myself in this uncharted water, it was going to be up to me to figure out the best way to navigate my way through it all with nothing that I could remotely call previous experience. Based on what I'd heard, to make it official, it was going to be up to me to pop the question in the way that men ask women for their hands in marriage. I did not go as far as dropping down on one knee, but when the time felt right, I gathered my thoughts and nerves, and asked her if she would be my girlfriend; and when she told me yes, I was happy that the ice had been broken.

Having a girlfriend at 14 years old was not as easy as I thought it would be. Suddenly I had to think about things that I never had to think about before. Not only did I have to think about ways to not appear too dull, boring, goofy, or "square," but I had to come up with things to talk to her about. It were as if I had the proverbial tiger by the tail, and now that I did, I didn't quite know what to do with it. Very much aware of the possibilities, I was not sure of the lines to cross and not to cross having a girlfriend at the start of my teenage years. Though we had a good drug prevention class at 43, there was nothing that taught us anything about being a boyfriend. Then, trying to rely on the advice of my friends was not much help either. They were just as clueless as I was, despite the confidence that came with the misinformation they dispensed liberally on a regular basis. So using my best judgment, and playing it as respectfully as possible, I kissed her, put my arms around her, and danced with her, but that was as far as I took matters. More times than I care to remember, I was not sure of what to say or talk to her about. There were more than just a few moments of awkward silences, but I was still happy to know that I had a girlfriend. Having a girlfriend was something special for us guys, so in that regard I was sitting pretty, and it felt as if I were on top of the world.

But a few months later, and right when I was starting to feel comfortable in my role as a significant other, I was caught by surprise when she brought it all to an end. A friend of ours from the building brought the news to me one day. She told me that my girlfriend told her to tell me that it was quits. In shock and having no backup plan, I had to face the hard and cold fact that my first romantic encounter had run its course, fizzled out, and gone up in smoke. So now I was back to square one, sad, and without a girlfriend. It was a tough, but very good lesson about the not so warm and fuzzy side of this thing that we call love and romance. As easy, fun, and exciting as it was getting into, as I learned, it was not all that fun getting out of. Tough lesson though it was, I knew that she had her life to live, and I had my life to live too. So I was soon up, dusted off, back on my horse, and on to the next adventure of my jam-packed junior high school years.

Around and about this time, a new community center opened that was still yet another excellent addition to our beautiful neighborhood. It was called the Stone Gym Youth Center; and it was a hit for us from day one. It was a state-of-the-art community center that was affiliated with Morningside Heights' very popular Riverside Church. Stone Gym had a turntable connected to its public address system, and speakers hung from walls everywhere in the building. This gave us the thrill of playing basketball to the great (early sixties') music that was so popular at that time. The basketball court was downstairs and it had a glossy hardwood floor with colorful floor markings. The main court was full sized, and there were two additional baskets on each side of the gym. So six, three-on-three pickup games could be played at the same time. In a smaller room next to the gym there was an area set up for boxing. It had mats, a speed bag, and a punching bag. We even had a boxing coach from Jamaica named Bobo Rickley who taught us how to box. So along with learning how to box, we quickly learned what it feels like to have a boxing glove smash into the sides of our heads, or have it knock the wind out of us. Tired and struggling to hold our arms up after what seemed like an eternity of sparing, Bobo continued to encourage us to jab; he would say "Jobum mon jobum!"

Upstairs there was a recreational room and lounge where we played pool and ping-pong. Two doors in the lounge led to a balcony that overlooked the gym. On the balcony we played cards, listened to music, talked, and watched the basketball games going on in the gym below. At the other side of the lounge were a kitchenette, a locker room, and another room where the turntable and the public address system were kept. We played basketball for the first hour-and-a-half, then we went upstairs to spend the rest of the time in the lounge listening to music and playing table games until the center closed at 10:00 o'clock. We had parties at Stone Gym, and we even had a sleepover there once. The freedom and independence this sleepover provided us with may have been a little bit too stimulating for some of the guys. It took them forever to go to sleep and they ran around making noise late into the night. With Stone Gym's director upstairs, and trying desperately to get some sleep, his well-intentioned idea of a sleepover did not work out quite like he had planned. So this trial run failed, and squashed any idea of another Stone Gym sleep over in the future. Despite that slight transgression, the Stone Gym Youth Center provided paid jobs for many of us, and it was a good, fun, and safe place for us to go at night.

Going to and from Stone Gym, we walked by the old Julliard School of Music at the corner of Broadway and 122nd Street; currently the building is the home of the Manhattan School of Music. The Julliard

School of Music was founded in 1905, and is considered one of the most prestigious music conservatories in the world. With there being no top-flight music schools in the United States at that time, it was felt that far too many students from the United States were going to Europe to study music; so this paved the way for Julliard's inception.

The window to one of the practice rooms was right in the path that we took to and from Stone Gym. So from the sidewalk, we could look right down into one of the rooms to see the students practicing. One day someone would be playing a cello, and the next time someone else would be playing a piano, a set of timpani, or a violin. I used to stop for at least five minutes each time to get an eye and earful of these dedicated students working hard to sharpen their skills. After getting my fill, I'd meet everyone at Maria's at the bottom of the hill for a slice of pizza and a soda before calling it a night.

Some kids in our group took to banging on a man's door on our way home after the center closed. For most of us, this was not our idea of fun, but when we least expected it, someone would run over, pound on the man's door, and then take off running. As a result, the rest of us had no choice but to take off running too. So, if the police had been waiting at the bottom of the hill one of those times, we would have all been in trouble. The interesting thing about this was that the man never came out to complain, nor did he call the police. Instead, he would just wait for the banging to start. Then he would fling his door open to let his huge dog out to chase everyone down the street. By some miracle, no one was ever bitten, but it did become a regular game of cat and mouse between the kids, the man, and his dog. It seemed as if the man was just as entertained by the rogue behavior as the few kids who got it all started.

Grant's Tomb is a block or two from Stone Gym. So on warm and balmy summer nights, it was our favorite place to spend time before going home. Though it hardly sounds like a place for a group of kids to enjoy a night out, the area is so beautiful, safe, clean, and isolated that it was a perfect refuge for us. It has a spectacular view of the Hudson River, its boats, and New Jersey with its lights that twinkled like diamonds in the night. With us guys becoming increasingly interested in the girls and vice versa, Grant's Tomb gave us the perfect place to escape the watchful eyes of parents, neighbors, and the thousands of windows looking down on us in any of our front or back yards. So, in our secluded hideaway, we were able to work on smoothing out the rough edges that came with being teenagers trying to sharpen our social skills.

Much like having a girlfriend, smoking cigarettes seemed to place guys higher up in the neighborhood's male pecking order. While watching a friend blow smoke rings and puff smoke from his nose on our way from Stone Gym one night, I asked him if I could give it a try. He gave his cigarette to me, and I put it up to my lips, took in a puff of smoke, held the smoke in my mouth, and blew it out. After seeing smokers appearing to enjoy their cigarettes so much for so long, I was surprised that the taste was as bad as it was. Then I asked him if that was all there is to smoking. In reply, he told me that I didn't do it the right way, and that I needed to inhale the smoke to fully enjoy a cigarette. After that he told me to take in a breath of air while the smoke is in my mouth; nothing seemed too difficult to me about that, so I continued by giving it a try. Following my young smoking instructor's words to the letter, I took in a long drag of smoke and watched the ashes light up and glow at the front end of the cigarette. I held the smoke in my mouth, and then I chased it down with a deep breath of air, expecting to experience smoking pleasure for the first time. Instead of feeling anything that I could call pleasurable, I felt something else. For starters, it felt to me as if the world and time had stood still for several long seconds. This was a harbinger, and only a small taste of things to come. I am not sure of exactly what it was, but something else happened that made it seem as if I had lost my eyesight for that same amount of time, too. While all of this was happening, I felt a crushing pain in the middle of my chest that felt as if I had been kicked by a horse. Then next, I found myself doubled over in a severe coughing spell with smoke, and just about everything else spewing from my nose and mouth. It took a full minute before I'd even started to recover. Having had such a bad reaction to my first attempt at smoking, anyone's guess would likely be that I put an end to it all right then and there. But as counterintuitive as it was on my part, I didn't. I took it as a challenge to be able to inhale the smoke without coughing, as I saw so many smokers do. Then two nights later, while standing in the same place as before (right in front of Julliard's music school) with my same friend, I thought I'd give it another try. This time, I took in a much smaller puff of smoke and inhaled it. The taste was just as bad as before; I coughed and felt the pain in my chest again, but it wasn't as bad as it was the first time. Then, two nights after that, I did it again, and for the first time I didn't cough or feel the pain in my chest. Other than the horrible taste, it felt as if I had taken in a breath of air. After that, I took another puff, inhaled the smoke, and even blew a smoke ring this second time. As I watched my perfect smoke ring drift away and disintegrate in mid-air, something clicked in my head. Though it felt like an accomplishment to me at first, luckily I came to my senses and put an end to it right then and there. It started to feel like too much of a slippery slope that could have resulted in a bad and unhealthy habit. So, I stopped at that point, and I never touched a cigarette again.

Not only did we have Stone Gym and Grant's community center, but during the summer months, P.S. 125 had a free summer day camp program too. It seemed as if a group of brilliant social engineers had been called together to design our neighborhood. We were served lunch, and they had table games there for us too. What we enjoyed most about P.S. 125's day camp was being able to swim there five days a week. With the summer months being as hot as they were, we swam all the time. Like Stone Gym, P.S. 125's day camp was free, so my friends and I were in water almost as much as we were on dry land, and I always found myself trying to shake swimming pool water out of my ears. Before learning how to swim, we were happy to splash and play at the shallow end of the pool. But by us spending so much time in the pool, it would have been practically impossible for us not to learn how to swim. First, I learned to lie out face down on the water's surface while holding my breath. Then I learned to stroke my arms and kick my legs; and before long, I knew how to swim.

We used to line up at the pool's door every morning, eagerly waiting for the pool attendant, Mr. Malloy, to let us in. On one of those mornings, it was clear that Mr. Malloy had "tied one on" pretty well the night before. So, with red eyes, an unsteady hand, and the unmistakable scent of alcohol following him around, he was having a hard time finding the keyhole with his key. Watching him poke at every part of the door around the keyhole, it was so funny to us that we could hardly contain our half-stifled giggles. When he saw us laughing, he didn't find our reaction to it all that funny or cute. He stopped poking at the door, glared at us angrily and asked, "What are you kids laughing about?" Then in an instant, all of the giggling stopped, and rightfully so. Mr. Malloy was the imposing autocrat who called all the shots at P.S. 125's swimming pool, and he could determine who would and would not swim for the day. Since none of us wanted to test him on it, we straightened up quickly by wiping every trace of a smile or laughter from our faces. Eventually, and after a few more attempts, he was able to find the keyhole and get the door open.

While in the locker room another time, two or three prankster friends of mine, aided by a lapse in good judgment on my part could have resulted in me being banned from swimming and summer day camp forever. They told me if I went into the girls' locker room and stood behind a wall just inside the door, I would be able to look inside without anyone knowing I was there. With my generally good sense of right and wrong badly impaired or wiped away completely by hearing this bit of news, it didn't take any further prompting on their part to get me to take the bait.

I pulled the door to the boys' locker room open and looked around to be sure that Mr. Malloy was nowhere nearby. Then when I saw that the coast was clear, like a thief in the night (and a creepy one at that), I tiptoed across the hall and quietly pushed the door to the girls' locker room open. I looked inside and saw that everything was exactly the way it had been described to me. What I didn't know was that my friends were right behind me. While I stood in the doorway, having serious doubts about what I was doing, one or two of them gave me a hard shove; and in the process, my feet became entangled or caught against a floor mat or the door's raised threshold. This sent me crashing to the floor of the girls' locker room. Then, very loudly, my (so-called) friends slammed the door shut on me. Terrified, I jumped up, ran back to the door, and pulled at the handle; but they were holding it shut from the other side. So there was nothing I could do; banging on the door, or calling to them to let me out were not options. At that point, all I could do was be as quiet as possible, sweat bullets, hope Mr. Malloy didn't catch me, hope that none of the girls came to the door to leave, and hope that none of them heard all the noise we made.

I was sure that I was going to be caught and that my summer day camp days would soon be over. As much as we loved swimming, being kicked out would have been one of the worst things that could have happened to any of us; and being kicked out for what I did made it even worse. As it turned out, no one heard the noise or knew I was there. It suddenly occurred to me how odd it was that this place that I was so curious about a minute or two earlier had suddenly become the last place I wanted to be on earth. An agonizing ten seconds passed with my mind racing as I tried to figure a way out of this fix. Then in a last ditch effort, I went back to the door, pulled at the handle again, and to my surprise and relief the door flew open. Then, as fast as my legs would carry me, I took off running across the hall and back into the boys' locker room. There I found my friends on the floor stretched out, doubled over, and holding their stomachs with tears in their eyes from laughing so hard. Seeing them have such a good laugh at my expense, and relieved that I had not been caught, as angry as I was, all I could do was laugh along with them and assure them that some form of payback was already in the pipeline and on the way.

With my swimming improving every day, I soon wanted to take my deep-water test. Passing the test would make it possible for me to swim at the deep side of the pool. The deep side of the pool was only six feet deep, but to us kids, six feet seemed like the murky and mysterious depths of the Hudson River. To pass I had to jump into the water, swim the length of the pool and back (roughly one-hundred feet each way). Then I had to tread water for a minute. When I was sure that I could do it, I took the test and passed it on my first try.

On that same day, while in the middle of the deep section of the pool, out of the corner of my eye, I saw a guy run toward the pool's edge, take a wild flying cannonball-styled leap into the water, and land on top of me. This caused my head to go below the water's surface briefly. It was something that I should have been able to recover from quickly and easily. But having just passed my deep-water test, I'd not become fully comfortable being in deep water, and I panicked. Rather than composing myself, getting my bearings, treading water, and swimming to the edge of the pool to climb out, I started to thrash around in the water helplessly with my head bobbing below the surface while I sucked water into my nose and mouth.

One of the more experienced swimmers dove into the water to try to pull me out, but because I was so panic stricken, I put him in danger, too, by the way I grabbed and clutched at him in all out panic mode. So, for his own safety, he had to abort his noble rescue mission. I do not know where the lifeguard was while all of this was happening, and Mr. Malloy was still nowhere to be found. There was a long metal pole with a hook at its end for situations like this, but no one thought to get it to fish me out of the water.

So there I was kicking, splashing, and fighting for my life as I continued to ingest water with everyone watching helplessly. Splashing and flailing around as much as I did with my eyes closed, I had no idea that my thrashing had carried me from the middle of the pool to the pool's edge, and right in front of the ladder that is used to climb out of the water. Then by sheer luck I opened my eyes, saw where I was, stopped my flailing, casually reached up, and climbed out of the pool.

Badly shaken and exhausted, I went to the seats at the side of the pool to take a minute to get myself collected. As soon as I sat down, all of the water that I had swallowed and sucked into my nose surged up, out of my mouth, and onto the tiled floor, and I started to feel better. After that, I started to look around for the guy who did the cannonball leap on top of me. Someone told me that they saw him hurry off to the locker room to leave, after realizing what he had done. I went to the locker room, and caught him right after he finished getting dressed. With wet hair and partially wet street clothes, he was on his way to the exit door when I saw him. Before he was able to leave, I ran over and stopped him. I asked him why did he jump on top of me and if he thought it was funny. Without much of an answer or explanation for what he did, I thumped him with a shot to his chest right before he left. He walked away possibly with my knuckle print on his chest, and I walked away still a bit shaken, but very lucky that I didn't drown on the same day I passed my deep-water test. Because I knew that it was nothing more than me panicking, my enthusiasm for swimming did not change at all. The next day, I was right back at the pool's door, bright and early, enthusiastically waiting for Mr. Malloy to come to let us in. It were as if my near-drowning incident had never happened.

My mother's best friend's daughter, Yvonne, was always a very special person for me. She was my guardian angel who helped me with my summer work assignment when I came close to being held back to repeat the fifth grade. In every sense of the word, Yvonne was like a doting big sister to me. She used to call me "Skigg," and she always wanted to know what I was up to and how I was doing. While completing her last-minute shopping one Christmas Eve, she came by to see if I wanted to tag along with her. We went to the Midtown department stores as she picked up her last few gifts. It was fun hanging out with her and mingling with the New York City last-minute Christmas shoppers. When she finished shopping, she treated me to a pizza and a soda before taking me home. This was typical of the nice things that Yvonne and her mother did for me all the time. I realize, now, much more than before that there was something that they both liked about me.

This time, Yvonne gave me a job referral. She knew two women who owned a florist in Harlem who needed someone to do their deliveries. When Yvonne told me about the job, I went to meet the two women, and they hired me right away. They were a kind of grumpy pair, and I never felt a sense of warmth from them towards me. But because it was a job that allowed me to spend most of my time out of the shop, I was not overly bothered by their less than sunny dispositions. Additionally, the job gave me a chance to earn a little money during the summer. During my time working there, they never really said much to me unless it had something to do with directions or instructions on a delivery. Their reputation as florists must have been good, because they received orders from all over the New York City area. So with a subway map and direction, I traveled all over NYC's five boroughs making deliveries to a wide assortment of clients. I was a responsible kid, so each order made it to its destination on time and in the same excellent condition it was in when I carried it out of the shop.

The freedom that the job offered was nice, and I enjoyed discovering so many new, different, and interesting parts of the New York City area. But what bothered me most about the job was making deliveries to so many funeral homes. With the summer in full bloom, and being my favorite time of the year, I found these dark, sad, and somber places very depressing. Even with the money I earned, these deliveries were putting a real damper on my otherwise fun-filled summer vacation.

Nonetheless, I kept my shoulder to the wheel for as long as I could before throwing the towel in. The breaking point came for me on one delivery in particular. When I arrived, the woman at the front desk was talking on the telephone and filing her nails. While I stood waiting for her, she didn't seem the least bit concerned about making me wait until she finished talking. So after a few minutes, I interrupted her and asked if I could leave the wreath with her to take upstairs later. On that day, I was not particularly up for seeing another lifeless body stretched out before a set of folding chairs. In no way was I rude, nor did I think that I had asked too much of her either. But instead of agreeing to do it (as I thought she would) she excused herself from the person she was talking to, covered the receiver, and snapped at me harshly: "Oh boy, just go on up there and take that wreath, that body is not going to do anything to you!" I took the wreath upstairs, but after that delivery and taking everything into consideration (including my two grumpy bosses), I decided that I'd had enough and never went back, hoping to enjoy what was left of my summer vacation.

Learning to fish and fishing was another way I spent my summer months during my junior high school years. My mother's brother (who my siblings and I called "Uncle B.") loved fishing, and he took me out one day to show me how it's done. With the Hudson River only five blocks from my building, it took no more than a ten-minute walk to find a place to sit out on the waterfront, to cast my line into the water, and escape the hustle and bustle of the city for a few hours. It didn't take long for me to realize how relaxing and enjoyable fishing is, and the perfect way it is to pass the time with my friends on hot summer days.

As the novelty of fishing started to wear off, there were several things about it that started to bother me. Despite considering myself a halfway devoted fisherman, I didn't like killing the sandworms and bloodworms that we used for bait. Nor did I like their pinchers that could pinch right into a finger. Additionally, the idea of eating fish that eat worms did not sit that well with me either, after making that connection. Then too, pulling fish out of the water with my hook caught in their mouths and seeing them flopping around and suffering bothered me too. Thinking about it now, I am glad that I had that kind of concern for other living creatures at that age. But at the same time, my thoughts were kind of self-serving, too. With my wild and weird imagination being what it was, I wondered how I would like biting into a sandwich to find a hook caught in my mouth that dragged me away from our table, away from my family, out the door, down the street, and into the river to be torn apart and eaten by a school of hungry fish. Not only that, but I was not all that crazy about being near so many airborne fishhooks and (2-ounce) sinkers flying around my head. Nonetheless, I still enjoyed the other aspects of fishing, so it continued to have a certain amount of appeal for me. Now, with these mixed feelings, there was a sense of excitement for me whenever I saw or felt a tug on my line. But it would all end when I reeled in my catch, and saw it flopping around, suffering, and struggling to survive on dry land.

In spite of it all, I continued fishing until I noticed something else that particularly bothered me about fishing in the Hudson River. This was a bit too much for me to ignore, and it was the deal breaker for me. Up the river and less than a half mile away, there was a warehouse that belonged to the city's sanitation department. While out on the 125th Street Pier with my line in the water, I started to see garbage trucks arrive, one after the other, to drop off garbage at this warehouse. Then, soon after, I would see large flat barges carrying huge piles of garbage out to the middle of the river from the warehouse and tilt to the side to dump tons of garbage into the water. No one else seemed to notice it or care, but it bothered me.

Primarily we caught striped bass and eels in the Hudson River. Then whenever we lowered our crabbing baskets into the water, crabs were plentiful too. I do not know about striped bass, but with crabs and eels being the scavengers they are, it only makes sense to me now that they would thrive the way they did in such garbage-strewn water. So after seeing garbage dumped into the water and seeing a fishhook pierce a man's scalp, I was done with fishing, and on to the next thing that caught my attention as I wrapped up my junior high school years.

4.

A New Beat
for the Neighborhood,
Harlem, and New York City

During my last year of junior high school, something changed my life just about as much as our move to Morningside Heights. Hot on the heels of the popular "American" music of the early 60's, another style of music emerged and hit New York City, Harlem, and our neighborhood with a sizable impact. It was unlike anything I'd ever heard. My sister played it for me the first time I heard it, and offered to show me how the dance to it is done. Challenged in many ways when it came to dancing, I was not all that enthusiastic about trying to learn yet and still another new dance. But I played along halfheartedly, and got the hang of it pretty quickly, much to my surprise.

We called it Latin music at that time, but now it is more commonly known as salsa. Rooted in the popular music and dance of Cuba, I don't know how or when my sister learned about it, but she knew the dance very well when she taught me. She had a way of bringing good music home all the time. By way of her wide-ranging tastes in music, I learned of South Africa's Miriam Makeba, Cuba's Mongo Santamaria, Nigeria's Michael Olatunji, Sly and the Family Stone, and Isaac Hayes.

After this dance lesson, almost everything about me changed. I started to eat, sleep, drink, walk, and breathe "Latin music." I worked on my Latin dance steps all the time as the twist, the two-step, the slop, and the mashed potatoes faded into the background for me. Then before long I'd become a regular and well-known customer at all the record stores on 125th Street. I combed through their record bins looking for Latin 45-rpm singles and 33½-rpm albums, and I bought practically everything the clerks played for me. As soon as the clerks saw me, their eyes would light up, because they knew they had at least two or three sales. The record stores used to blast Latin music from speakers out onto 125th Street; and since there was always something good playing, it never failed to draw me inside to find out the names of the various bands and recording artists.

My friend, Steven Wright, told me more recently that he always knew if I were home or not before he got to our door. If he heard the music when he stepped off the elevator, he knew I was there. My sister once told me that I played a song called "Descarga Palmieri" so much that it is forever carved into her memory. As loudly and as much as I played my records, it was a miracle that my neighbors never complained. Had that been the case, I don't know what I could have done. This was long before headphones, and I was too far gone at that point. The music had become almost as important to me as air, food, and water. So I played it cranked way up in order to hear its many fascinating details. I played it in the morning while I got ready for school, thought about it on my way to school and while I was in class. I played it again, first thing, when I got home, and I listened to it while doing my homework. Listening to it gave me goose bumps, and whenever I heard something that I particularly liked, it made me break out into cold sweats. I think my neighbors liked the music, and I know that my mother liked it too. Being a piano player, the chances were good that the exciting piano playing caught her ear. As I recall, there was only one or two times that she asked me to turn it down a little. Caught in the throes of one of my overly enthusiastic listening sessions, I had gone a bit too far with the volume control knob.

While at Grant's Tomb with a friend of mine, a boat on the Hudson River blasted its horn. After hearing it, my friend and I looked at each other. Then we started to laugh; we laughed because we knew we were thinking the same thing. The horn blast sounded like the opening bass and piano note to Ray Barretto's mega hit tune, El Watusi (that he roundly won NYC's Latin music lovers and dancers over with). So for a second or two, we thought we were going to hear a highly amplified version of El Watusi played from the boat. It would have been nice to hear such a popular song at that volume, coming from the middle of the Hudson River so unexpectedly; but the boat blasted its horn only one time. Then there was silence as the boat continued on its way into the night. So not only was Latin music everywhere, but it was causing me to hear it when it was not even being played.

Large numbers of people from the neighborhood, Harlem, and NYC were caught up in this musical whirlwind, and particularly was my generation of African-American teenagers. Despite the language gap, the African elements of the music must have touched us in some kind of visceral way, without us realizing it. Then along with that, the music is so good that it has a way of winning people over very quickly. Some may be surprised to hear that Latin music was played in many parts of Harlem where, until that time, only African-American styles of music were played. In the same way that rap and hip-hop have enthralled, captivated, and defined several generations more recently, "Latin music" did the same for a very large number of people prior to and during the early 60s in the NYC area. Then when it occurred to me that Latin music would be yet another way to help me with my Spanish, I knew that my sister had set me out and onto a unique and interesting path. The idea of learning Spanish while dancing to and enjoying such great music was something that was almost too good to be true. So, whenever there were words, phrases, or song titles that I didn't understand, I'd find one of my Spanish-speaking friends to translate the meanings for me.

As Latin music continued to take hold, I either danced or thought about dancing all the time. When there was no music, I sang the rhythms and did my best to sing the words while I worked on my dance steps. Then if there were no girls to dance with, my friends and I would line up side-by-side, and we worked on perfecting the coordinated, complex, and choreographed dance steps that we had a lot of fun creating and practicing. Other times we would dance with each other. My mother liked the dance so much that she sometimes asked my sister and me to do dance demonstrations for her friends while she watched with a smile and the very clear look of a parent's approval on her face. After playing basketball at Stone Gym, my friends and I would go upstairs to the lounge, blast the music, and we danced until the center closed. So as much as my ears perked up whenever I heard the voices of Sarah Vaughn, the Everly Brothers, Jackie Wilson, Dell Shannon, or (East Harlem's) Bobby Darin on the radio, Latin music came along and swept me off my feet too, right along with just about everyone else.

With the shifting political winds in Cuba sending Cubans to the United States during the late fifties and early sixties like never before, it only added fuel to the fire of this musical upsurge. Arriving with their colorful culture, customs, music, and larger-than-life personalities, the floodgates for Latin music into the United States were kicked wide open. A style of music called charanga was probably at its height in popularity in Cuba at that time, and this migration resulted in an explosion of charanga bands in New York City.

During that time, one of the very popular Latin bands in NYC was a charanga band led by an energetic and charismatic guy named Johnny Pacheco. Johnny Pacheco was born in the Dominican Republic, and he came to the United States when he was 11 years old. Though from the Dominican Republic, "Pacheco" had long loved Cuban music. When the final book on Latin music is written, Johnny Pacheco's name and influence will factor into it in a very big way. "Pacheco" became a popular icon, seemingly, overnight; and, as far as I was concerned, he was the personification of musical excellence. He captivated almost an entire generation with his flute playing, his highly charged band, and his music. Though Herbie Mann was a popular flute player during that time, I was probably Johnny Pacheco's biggest fan. When I learned about him, he had already started to win New Yorkers over with many of his recordings: Acuyuye, Alto Songo, Agua de Clavelito, and Suavito were only a few.

Adding to Johnny Pacheco's mystique and appeal, for me, was the fact that he didn't play the more familiar modern (silver) Boehm-styled flute. Instead, he played a vintage wooden flute from the mid 1800s that

I had never seen before. To me they looked like 2-feet-long cuts of dark sugarcane, and they have several colloquial names. Most often they are called charanga flutes, five-key flutes, or Cuban flutes. Some call them simple-system flutes, and I have heard some call them "palos," (or sticks in English). They are so simply made that they look as much like sticks as musical instruments. Not particularly well-documented instruments, information about these flutes is sketchy at best. But they are more officially known as Meyer-system flutes. Despite their poor documentation and somewhat primitive look, they are actually quite sophisticated, and without a doubt, there is something uniquely pleasing about their very distinctly sweet sound. Regarding the names "charanga flute" and "Cuban flute," these labels are a bit misleading. First of all, they were made in Germany, France, and England, and not Cuba. Secondly, they were originally used in old styles of classical music long before they became fixtures in popular Cuban dance music. I saw a picture of one made of clear glass that was custom made for Napoleon Bonaparte (who was purportedly a big flute enthusiast).

Made primarily of granadilla, ebony, cocus wood, cocobolo wood, or rosewood, they look a lot like the wooden flutes used in early Irish folk music. But the flutes used in Cuban music have only five, or six keys at most. The type of wood these flutes are made of is very special, and, more often than not, is from the mpingo tree. The mpingo tree grows in the seasonably dry regions of East Africa. Conditions are ideal for the mpingo tree in Tanzania, Senegal, Mozambique, and Eritria. The wood from the mpingo tree is called African black wood or African hard wood, and the mpingo tree is called the "Tree of Music." In one of its pre-flute stages, I saw a block of mpingo wood that had been honed into a perfect cylinder; and, because of its density, it did not, at all, look or feel like wood. It actually looked and felt like a lead pipe. The wood's density and its natural oils protect it from moisture and parasites, and its density also causes these types of wood to sinks in water; they are even known for surviving forest fires. Given their unique characteristics, they are ideal for flutes, clarinets, and oboes. Purportedly, the wood from the mpingo tree commands the highest price for timber worldwide, and it is harvested after no less than 70 to 100 years of growth. Cocus wood, on the other hand, grows in Cuba, Jamaica, and in other parts of the Caribbean.

During and after the Haitian slave revolt, many French and African descendants fled Haiti, and migrated to the east coast of Cuba; and in the process hundreds (if not thousands) of these flutes found new homes for themselves there. In Cuba, they were used in symphony orchestras, small string ensembles, and other types of concert music. But when metal became flute makers' raw material of choice, many of these wooden flutes were abandoned by flute players to take advantage of the new trend in flute playing and the technological advancements achieved in flute making. On the other hand, flute players who played the earlier forms of charanga (charanga francesa and danzon) continued using these wooden flutes, and it was a good thing that they did. Had they abandoned the wooden flutes too, these beautiful instruments would have likely gone extinct, and may have never been seen or heard from again. As far as I know, charanga, charanga francesa, danzon, salsa, and classical music are the only styles of music that these flutes have been used in. So now, instead of being reduced to landfill, there are a surprisingly large number of them still being played in Cuban music presently. Given the very limited information about them, it is practically impossible to quantify how many have been made or how many are still around; but I can say that there are quite a few presently. Not only that, but it is anyone's guess as to how many are under beds in Cuba and around the world, collecting dust, since their previous owners played them last. In terms of documentation, these flutes were greatly overshadowed by (one of its forerunners) the very popular Baroque flute. As a result, these five-key French (German and English-made) "Cuban flutes" are practically unknown; and for all intent and purposes, these flutes are the unsung heroes of the flute family. Cuban five-key flute players were on to something, and must have recognized the tonal quality of what they had. The timbre of these flutes is much better suited for Cuban music. Articulated forcefully, percussively, and at the top end of the instrument's range in popular Cuban dance music, the sound created by these types of wood is not as shrill and cutting as metal. It's sound is warmer, sweeter, more round, and it seems to be a much better match for the (wooden) violins and cellos that are used in charanga, charanga francesa, and danzones. These flutes are, essentially, a cross between the Baroque flute and the modern Boehm silver flute; so they have a little bit of both eras. Made of wood, they have the warmth and sweetness of (the wooden) Baroque flutes, but at the same time (like the modern flutes) they are fully chromatic. As a result, they can play every note and scale that the modern silver flute plays, in spite of how simple they look. Then too, by being handmade, visually, they are truly fine-crafted works of art; and as it seems, these flutes were made with aesthetics in mind, just about as much as sound. Unique and distinct as rare instruments go, they are somewhat of an exotic mix between flutes, clarinets, and oboes. So based on appearance alone, if there were ever such a thing as a "magic flute," I would say that five-key flutes would (I have plenty of photos of them on my website: twoneighborhoodsinharlem.com)

The flute players who played them in Cuban music were not only talented and wise, but they were resourceful too. They have managed to stretch these flutes to their limits in terms of what they can do with them. By trial and error they figured out the fingering positions for very high notes that were not needed or ever used in concert music. Additionally, they widened the tone hole and slid the (cork) stopper in closer to the tone hole too. These changes made it possible for them to reach notes that are well up into the piccolo's range. As a result they have a three-and-a-half octave range that starts at "D" (right above middle C) and can reach high "G," three-and-a-half octaves above middle C. Though the Meyer-system flutes made in England and Germany are excellent instruments, the ones made in France (hence the ones that ended up in Cuba) were particularly well made. So Cuba got a very good end of the deal when it came to the dispersal of these three types of flutes out to the rest of the world.

So not only was I taken by Latin music and the charanga style in particular, but I liked the way these flutes were used to complement, enhance, and embellish this exciting music. These Cuban-styled flute players had a way of getting a sound from these instruments that connected with me quickly; and though usually used in a completely different context, I found their sound to be raw, sweet, and organic. I was hooked as soon as the sound hit my eardrums, and I seemed to never be able to get enough of this compelling sound. So when I was not working on my dance steps, I used to sit practically inside our stereo cabinet listening to the twists and turns made by these incredibly agile and talented flute players. Then while I listened, I read the liner notes on the album covers, and gazed hypnotically at the musicians and the unique collection of instruments that make this great music possible.

Speaking of five-key flutes and the impact that they were starting to have on me, something else wrapped up my junior high school years on a particularly high, sweet, and beautiful grace note. I did not win any of J.H.S. 43's scholastic achievement awards (I can assure you that), but I did manage to walk away with something that was even more valuable, rewarding, satisfying, and meaningful to me. My classmates and I learned that our prom was going to be held at the very high-end Americana Hotel in Midtown Manhattan. The prom was organized and held in conjunction with other junior high schools throughout the city. There was nothing particularly special, for me, about that, but what really caught my attention was a rumor that a Latin band was going to play. As big a fan as I'd become, I very much looked forward to seeing a Latin band play for the first time. Then to top that off, word had it that the featured attraction was going to be Johnny Pacheco and his band.

Being that it was a junior high school prom, rather than a dance that was open to the general public, there were no flyers or posters to corroborate any of the rumors that swirled around us. So everything we heard about it was by word of mouth. Nonetheless, I was still very excited at just the idea of seeing Johnny Pacheco play live and in person. As the night of the prom approached, I was brimming with anticipation, but careful not to get my hopes up too high.

Several months before the prom, Johnny Pacheco played a weeklong engagement at the Apollo Theater, and for some reason, I didn't go. Even more remarkable than that is the fact that I do not even remember why I didn't go. Since I lived only three blocks from the Apollo Theater, getting there would have not been a problem for me at all; and along with that, I could have easily scratched up the money from my mother for something that special. A classmate of mine did see Pacheco's Apollo debut performance, and excitedly gave us a glowing review of what he saw and heard.

This engagement was momentous because it was the first time that a Latin band had ever played at the Apollo Theater. Coupled with that, an entire city of Latin music dancers and lovers seemed to have been completely taken under Johnny Pacheco's spell. My classmate told me that Johnny Pacheco and his band "turned the place out" (an expression that we used to use). Listening to him talk about what he saw, it sounded like nothing less than a command performance. He told us too that Pacheco's flute playing was unlike anything he had ever seen or heard. Hearing this made me regret missing Pacheco's Apollo performance even more, but I knew that I would be at the Americana Hotel bright and early with every hope that Pacheco would be on the bill for the night.

On the evening of the prom, my friends and I still had no confirmation about who was going to play. But I do remember the first part of the evening very well. At sunset, on the evening of the prom, my friends and I waited for the bus on Riverside Drive, and I clearly remember taking note of the beautiful evening and perfect spring weather. The orange-colored sunlight reflected up against surface of the Hudson River, and it added an unusually beautiful tint to air and to everything else that it touched. It was one of those balmy spring New York City evenings and sunsets that I have always liked. The water appeared to be as still as a sheet of glass, so the stage was set for a night to remember, or for one of the biggest disappointments of all times.

After our short ride to Midtown, we entered the plush hotel's fancy ballroom, and as if drawn in by a magnet, I found myself standing at the front of the stage. The stage was about 5-feet high, and on it I saw a conga drum on a conga drum stand, a set of timbales, three or four violins, amplifiers, a bass, and a piano. I knew that charanga bands use violins; so seeing the violins was a good sign for me. But if, in fact, Johnny Pacheco and his band were the featured performers for the evening was still the unanswered question.

Junior high school graduates from all over the city started to fill the ballroom soon after. While waiting for the music to start, I could feel the energy, excitement, and anticipation build. Given the level of excitement

I felt, it is very likely that I felt it more than anyone else. Before the music started, the master of ceremonies came out to welcome us. He made a few cursory announcements and introduced the band. I do not remember all of his exact words, but I do clearly remember hearing him say: "Now ladies and gentlemen, for your listening and dancing pleasure, the Americana Hotel proudly presents Mr. Johnny Pacheco and his band." After that, everyone applauded, cheered, and whistled. While standing at the front of the stage, I felt my Latin music goose bumps rise up on my arms even before the music started. Approximately ten musicians walked out to take their places on stage. As surreal as it all seemed, it hit me all at once that I was finally going to see a Latin band play for the first time. Then most of all, I knew that I was finally going to get to see this iconic figure in action after seeing pictures of him on my album covers and hearing him play on my records all along.

Being every bit the showman he is, Johnny sauntered out to the front and center of the stage carrying his five-key flute. He wore a sharp tuxedo, and he did not appear to be much older than us teenagers in the crowd. He looked like a kid himself compared to many of his older band members. Already impressed by the instrument, seeing it right in front of me for the first time, it looked like a fancy scepter; and it also reminded me of a magic wand. Pacheco passed the flute back and forth between his hands while he bent down to banter with us excited kids as we stood at the front of the stage, wide eyed, while waiting for the music to start. He looked like a magician who was going to pull a rabbit from a silk top hat. His magnetism, easily, made him the center of focus, and he knew quite well how to play it up to make the most of his spectacular entrance.

With the preliminaries out of the way, like the conductor of a symphony orchestra holding a baton, Pacheco cued his airtight band into their first tune for the night. Then from that point on, it was bombs away; and it was clear that Pacheco and his band had come to light everyone and everything up. They torched the place as Pacheco overwhelmed everyone and whipped the crowd into a dancing frenzy. Like a pinball, he was all over the place as he punctuated the notes, melodies, and flute licks he thrilled the dancers with. For me, it was the musical ride of a lifetime, and it is easily one of the very best musical performances I have ever seen. It's too bad that there were no cell phone (video) cameras at that time; it was a show that I would give anything to see again, or be able to show to people now. Pacheco sang, danced, leaped into the air, played his flute, and won the crowd over with both his music and showmanship. As much as I enjoy dancing, I didn't dance once. Overwhelmed by the performance, I was frozen in one spot at the front of the stage as I watched Pacheco, and each musician's every move.

When the first set ended, I made my way through the crowd to find a pen and a piece of paper. Then I came back to the front of the stage to find Pacheco, and I asked him for his autograph. As I approached him I was unsure of how he would feel about me asking for his autograph. It was pretty clear to me how engaging he was on stage while facing the public, but I had no idea of what he would be like, one on one, with me hounding him for his autograph. But I didn't really care; given the way that he had just electrified the ballroom, it would have not even bothered me if he had refused and brushed me off as pesky kid. Had that been the case (at the least, and for the record) I would be able to say that I spoke to him, and I would still be one of Pacheco's biggest fans. He had completely won me over with such an outstanding performance. After asking him, very graciously, he stopped what he was doing, took the pen and paper, and stylishly affixed his fancy, large, and looping autograph to it. Then he did a quick sketching of a flute under it and said something to me that seemed to go into one of my ears and quickly came out of the other one, before handing the pen and paper back to me. Though I do not remember what he said, I do know that it was funny, because I remember laughing after hearing it. But I was too awestruck to remember what it was that he said. Nonetheless, my already high opinion of Johnny Pacheco shot up even more.

After their first break they came back to play two more sets, and everyone danced right through to the last note. I, instead, soaked it all up from the front of the stage while keeping a close eye on his beautifully crafted flute. I studied the keys, the wood, the contours of the instrument's body, the five interconnecting parts, and the details of how he played it. Before seeing Pacheco play, I had given occasional and passing thoughts to playing or having a five-key flute of my own, but after seeing him play it in person, I was sure that I had to have one. So I made an extra effort to remember exactly what they look like.

As well as I remember the details of the first part of the evening and the show itself, I was so taken by the performance that I do not remember anything else that happened after that. I do know that no one left disappointed, but I do not remember how the prom ended, leaving the building, or our ride home. My best guess is that my friends and I talked excitedly about what we saw and heard; or, quite possibly, we could have ridden home stunned and in a blissful state of silent euphoria. I do know that I was on cloud nine. Pacheco's band, his music, and his percussive and melodic flute licks continued to resonate in my head for the next few days. Charanga has thrilled dancers in Cuba long before I heard it; so it was a lot for me to take in as a 14-year old kid.

I thought a lot about the recorder I played in elementary school, and I thought about the leap it would take for me to learn to play the "Cuban" styled charanga flute. Clearly there were enough similarities between the two instruments to know that the transition was indeed very possible. But one of the more obvious problems for me was the difficulty of producing a sound on this much more sophisticated and challenging instrument. Requiring only a puff of air to get a sound from a recorder, I knew that getting a sound from a transverse flute was going to take a precise and carefully directed stream of air. Nevertheless, the challenge did not seem insurmountable. Since I watched Pacheco so closely, I had a good idea of what I would need to do to get a sound from a "Cuban flute."

Then too, even more problematic for me than that was the likelihood of finding one of these rare instruments. I could have settled for a modern Boehm silver flute; by that time, I knew that several Cuban-styled flute players used them. Not only that, but a Boehm flute would have been very easy for me to find at any music store or pawnshop. But the authentic, wooden, Cuban-styled, five-key, charanga flute was the only type of flute that I was interested in. So if I were ever going to have the good fortune of doing what I saw Johnny Pacheco do that night, I knew that my work was indeed cut out for me.

After the prom I was on a roll again, and was drawn even more into Latin music's powerful and quickly widening vortex. I started to go to Latin dances and concerts everywhere. Next, I went to a dance at a large ballroom in Midtown called Manhattan Center, and four bands played that night. I might have been the youngest person there and probably should have not been allowed in, given that I was only 14 years old. Be that as it may, I saw Tito Rodriguez, Eddie Palmieri, Ray Barretto, and Joe Cuba play that night, and the cover charge was only $3.00. Presently, a dance on that order would easily cost $60 or $70, if not more. At this dance, I had the pleasure of seeing the flute players for both Eddie Palmieri and Ray Barretto's bands for the first time.

After that I saw Eddie Palmieri's debut performance at the Apollo Theater and again got an earful of his five-key flute player, Jorge Castro. At the start of the show there were no announcements made, and no one came out to introduce the band. But instead, they did something different that I thought was very nice. Before the show, my friends and I talked while we waited for the music to start. Then, out of nowhere, and catching us by surprise, we heard the piano introduction to Eddie Palmieri's opening tune. The theater was dark, and the curtains were still closed. As the rest of the band followed Eddie's lead into the song, a set of red stage lights came on slowly, casting silhouettes of the eight musicians against the closed curtains while they played. Then, the curtains were raised slowly. This made the start of the show that much more dramatic. My two friends and I had perfect balcony seats, so we were able to see everything very well. Quite naturally my eyes were drawn right to Eddie's flute player, Jorge Castro. I had never heard their opening song, but its title is "Tema Del Apollo" or Theme of the Apollo. It is a very tasteful blues-like cha-cha-cha that was written by Eddie Palmieri, specifically to open the show with. Along with that, it seemed to me to be a beautiful, classy, memorable, and fitting tribute by Eddie Palmieri to the grand and glorious Apollo Theater. Additionally, I saw it as a clear gesture of recognition and gratitude to the African-American people who had come to see the show and who supported him as much as we did. Hearing and seeing this dramatic start to the show, my Latin music goose bumps kicked in right away, and I broke out into one of my profuse cold sweats like never before. As did Johnny Pacheco and his band, Eddie Palmieri, his flute player, and his band tore into their performance too and practically knocked me off my seat repeatedly throughout the show.

5

A Thrilling Ride: the Blazing Fast 8th Ave. "A" Train

Before this exciting finish to my junior high school years, it was time for me to choose a high school, and Charles Evans Hughes High School was where I decided to go. Be it my mother's intuition, apprehension, or whatever it was, she had a different take on things. Apparently, she sensed something troubling about my high school choice, because she switched my registration to another school without saying anything to me about it. Not only that, but she switched me to Dewitt Clinton High School which was an all boys' school in the Bronx. I don't know why, nor did I ask her about it. My sister was going to go to Walton (the all-girls' sister school to Dewitt Clinton), so it is likely that she wanted to keep us closer together. Whatever it was, I was looking forward to going to Hughes while having no idea that my plans had been derailed, leaving me on a beeline to Dewitt Clinton.

I didn't mind going to school in the Bronx, but the last place I wanted to spend my high school years was at an all boys' school. So my mother's plan was a big problem for me. I found out about what she did by seeing a letter that welcomed me to Dewitt Clinton during the summer. However, fortunately for me, my mother didn't have that side of her plan covered. So after reading the letter, without saying a word, I switched my registration back to Hughes.

Hughes was in the Chelsea section of Manhattan. Chelsea is just north of Greenwich Village and just south of Midtown. The blazing fast 8th Ave. "A" train got me there in no time. Sometimes I could take the #1 Broadway local train if I left home early enough, but I liked the way the A-train boldly blasts through the tunnel like an underground rocket as it quickly bypasses all of the local stops, hurtling its way up and down the middle express train tracks. I usually made it a point to ride in the lead car, and I stood at the front window (imagining how fun it would be to be at the controls). From the front window, and with much delight, I closely watched the A-train do what it was so well made to do. It is a thrilling ride, and it is much deserving of its high name recognition from Billy Strayhorn's popular composition and Duke Ellington's signature tune, "Take the 'A' Train."

High schools accepted students from all over the city, so I met interesting people from practically everywhere, students and teachers alike. A gym teacher named Mr. Levine was a perfect example of this. Noticing the way he was tapping his hands on the top of the piano in the auditorium, one day, made it clear to me that he knew a thing or two about Latin music and playing conga drums. Then when I asked him, he told me that he did. As a result, we connected quickly on this special thing that we had in common. He knew who all the musicians were, and we enjoyed talking about the exciting and fast growing New York City Latin music scene.

Two of my new classmates were connected to Latin music too. One was a guy named Nestor Sanchez. Nestor Sanchez was a budding singer who eventually went on to sing with Larry Harlow and his band. Nestor became known as "El Albino Divino" or "The Divine Albino." He loved Latin music, and he was an excellent singer; so we spent a lot of time talking about how nice it would be to play Latin music professionally. There was another classmate of mine named Victor Aviles. He didn't play music, but he told me that his father, Vatin Aviles, sang with Charlie Palmieri (Eddie Palmieri's older brother) in his charanga band, La Duboney.

My Spanish teacher's name was Mr. Feldstine, and he was a pretty interesting guy, to say the least. He was a bit on the brash, intense, eccentric, dramatic, theatrical, and dry humor sides of the human personality spectrum; and it seemed that he used the classroom to keep his acting chops and stage presence sharp. With one shirt collar up, the other one down, a crooked necktie carelessly tossed around his thick neck, and his hair standing on end, he was one of those teachers that you never forget. He wore the same suit every day, and it looked as if he had slept in it the night before. It was clear that he felt no pressure at all to fall in line with the high-styled fashionistas of NYC, and Peter Falk's character, Lieutenant Columbo, had nothing on him when it came to rumpled suits, worn out shoes, and eccentricity. So having him as a teacher added something different to the day, and to the process of learning Spanish.

Then there was Mr. Klinger; he was the school's musical director. He was a brilliant musician, music teacher, and conductor; and I am fondly reminded of Mr. Klinger whenever I see Bernie Sanders waving his arms and hands around when he speaks. Mr. Klinger had that same kind of energy, persona, and enthusiasm. Then along with that, he had such a perfect sense of pitch that he could sing a perfect A-440 for the Hughes orchestra to tune their instruments to. Though this kind of musical aptitude was probably expected of any high school music teacher, it impressed me to see it done for the first time. The quality of his orchestras, year in and year out, was always high. He made excellent choices of music to play, and his musicians always delivered by playing his selections well. Charles Evans Hughes' orchestra was so good that they could have played anywhere, and would have thrilled audiences each and every time. Mr. Klinger would have settled for nothing less. He was demanding, and he had a way of getting the best from each of his musicians.

Unlike the present-day slash and burn approach to budgeting that continues to destroy public school music programs now, our music program had everything it needed. The storage room was stocked piled with instruments, sheet music, and anything else needed to support a full orchestra. There were tubas, French horns, clarinets, trumpets, saxophones, kettledrums, upright basses, flutes, oboes, snare drums, bass drums, bassoons, music stands, and chairs. The storage room smelled like musical instruments, and Mr. Klinger played each one very well. The pockets of his blazers bulged with the mouthpieces to the various instruments. So if someone had trouble playing a part, he would rummage through his pockets to find the right mouthpiece. Then he would attach his mouthpiece to the student's instrument; and, without warming up, play the part flawlessly so the person could hear what it should sound like. After that, he would say something like this: "Geeez! Is there anything so hard about that?" Then as a word of advice on good musicianship to the entire orchestra, he would usually have a parting shot before moving on: "So you see, if you practice your parts and practice your instruments, there is no reason why your playing should sound like an ox on its death bed."

I played in the Hughes orchestra during the eleventh and twelfth grades, and I sat in the woodwind section, just below and right in front of Mr. Klinger. This was both good and bad. Occasionally, we would catch the spray from his mouth when he spoke, or the sweat from his brow while he conducted. Despite that small challenge, I had the good fortune of playing for and seeing an exciting conductor in action up closely, as he led us through our fine collection of songs. He held nothing back, and he had a way of letting it all fly during rehearsals and performances. He did whatever he could to deliver the best music possible, and he had a way of transforming written music into absolute treats for everyone's eyes and ears.

During the summer I was hired to work at a children's day camp that was a half block from my building. A city sponsored youth employment program provided the funding for these summer jobs. We took care of Puerto Rican and African-American children. We took them to the park, took them swimming, and we did all types of other recreational activities with them. The Puerto Rican children took a lot of pride and pleasure in helping me add to my ever-growing number of Spanish words and phrases.

As eager as I was to learn, I could tell that the kids enjoyed teaching me; and seeing the joy and enthusiasm on their small faces made it fun for me too. Along with taking care of the kids, we did any cleaning and painting that was needed; and I worked there for two of my high school summer vacations. We were paid $37.50 every two weeks, but without having to pay rent or any of the other usual adult living expenses, this relatively small amount of money provided us with plenty of pocket money during that time. Then most importantly, these jobs instilled a sense of responsibility, and good work habits in all of us at a very important time in our lives.

After a paycheck or two into my job, I had enough money saved to start my search for a flute. With John Coltrane, singlehandedly, being responsible for tenor saxophones selling like hotcakes and the Beatles causing perhaps twenty times as many guitars to fly out of music stores during that time, it was my luck to be taken by an instrument that was like trying to find a needle in a haystack. Making matters worse, I wanted one of those "Cuban flutes" so badly that I could almost taste it. I thought about them all the time; and while in class, I used to sketch them on pieces of paper so much that I'd gotten pretty good at it. Additionally, in the way that "wanna be" guitar players play "air guitar," I played air flute all the time.

There was a pawnshop less than a half-block from my building, and another pawnshop and a music store on the east side of 125th Street. All three sold flutes, but all I ever saw for sale at any of these places were Boehm silver flutes. Coming up empty handed in my initial search, I decided to try my luck with the cluster of music stores on 48th Street in Midtown. I was pretty sure I'd be able to find what I wanted there. Just about anything related to music could be found on this block-long stretch of seven or eight music stores. While there I worked my way from 6th to 7th Avenue, searching high and low, but all I ever saw were silver flutes.

Thinking that I had been to every store on the block, I was ready to call it quits for the day to try to come up with another plan, until I saw one last music store. I went inside and asked the clerk if he had any flutes.

He directed me to a large floor-level drawer. I went over, pulled it open, and saw that it was filled with used flutes, inside their cases. I inspected the contents of some seven or eight flute cases, and continued to come up with the same thing, Boehm silver flutes. But at the back of the drawer, I saw an old flute case that was very much unlike any of the other ones. I pulled the case out, opened it, and saw an old wooden flute inside. A charge of excitement shot through me when I saw it. Though made of the same type of wood I was looking for, upon closer inspection, I realized that it was not a Cuban flute. It was a Boehm-system flute made of ebony wood. Though interesting, nice, and a step closer to what I wanted, it was still not what I had in mind. Given the difficulty I'd been having with my search, I decided to settle on it until I was able to find what I really wanted. I took the case out of the drawer, carried it over to the clerk, and asked him for the price; then he told me that it costs $20. I then told him that I would be back to pick it up later, and asked him to hold it behind the counter for me.

At home I took $45 out of my dresser drawer. Since I had never played a flute, I needed a lesson book too. Then with every intention of celebrating my purchase with a slice of pizza and a soda, I knew that I would need the extra money. Back at the store, I asked the clerk for the flute. He reached for it and placed it on the counter. I handed him a twenty-dollar bill and waited for him to give me a receipt. Instead, he told me that he'd made a mistake earlier, and said that the flute actually costs $40. Perhaps seeing my excitement, he used it to get another $20 from me. Unfazed, I reached into my pocket and handed him my other $20 bill. I could have tried to bargain with him or complain about his sudden and arbitrary 100 percent price hike, but I wanted the flute. So despite his shifty business practice, $40 was still a good deal. Presently, these flutes can cost as much as $3,000. So, in the end, bringing the extra money was a good thing, and I was happy that I had a flute that was at least a step closer to the kind I really wanted. Then for a couple of dollars I bought a flute method book. The book was very good, and it had a chart inside with diagrams showing the fingering positions and the corresponding notes on, above, and below the five-line stave. It had plenty of songs and exercises in it, too. I taped the flute case and the book to the handlebar of my bicycle and rode home. Then too, I even had enough money left to celebrate my purchase with a slice of pizza and a soda at Maria's.

Finding a flute close to what I wanted was timely for me, because two friends of mine and I had already started to put a Latin band together, and the $5.00 metal fife that I'd been using was not loud enough to cut through with the sound that I needed and wanted. So now with my new flute, a flute method book, and plenty of dedication and determination, it was not long before I knew the fingering positions, the notes, the scales, and how to produce the bigger sound.

I do not remember exactly when it started, but somewhere during that time, the laundry list of sweets and other junk I feasted on regularly, started to catch up with me. It didn't cause me to gain weight, but right when girls were becoming more interesting to me than ever before, I broke out with a horrible case of acne. In my efforts to get the problem under control, I tried every type of acne medicine I could find; I washed my face more, drank more water, dabbed my face with rubbing alcohol, kept my hands away from my face, and nothing worked. One time, I tried a popular facial cream that someone suggested and swore by. Before going to bed, I smeared the stuff onto my face and went to sleep expecting to wake up to a new and improved complexion. But after looking in the mirror the next morning, much to my horror, I saw that my pimples had doubled or may have even tripled.

I have heard skin experts say that acne has nothing to do with what we eat. But based on an experiment I tried, I am amazed that this is said so often and said with so much authority and conviction. After trying everything I could think of to no avail, out of desperation I decided to try to do something about my eating to see if that would help. So for about a month, I cut the junk out completely. Then, much to my relief, I realized that I had found the remedy that had eluded me for so long, and the cause of my skin problem. Whenever hit by one of my cravings for candy, ice cream, cake, cookies, or soda, I bought and ate a ripe red apple instead, and within days my face cleared up. I continued to replace the candy and junk food with apples, and my face remained free from the horrible pimples that troubled me for so long. Then due to a false sense of security and a moment or two of temptation, after a month of faithfully eating apples, I lapsed back into my old bad eating habits again. Then before I knew it, my pimples had returned with a vengeance. Having the taste of the sugar, chocolate, or whatever else on my tongue again, my sweet tooth had become reactivated, and I found it impossible to gather the fortitude I needed to regain control of it.

In spite of my embarrassing skin problem and much to my surprise, I learned once again that if I played my cards right, I was only a step or two away from having my second girlfriend. With my first girlfriend not speaking to me anymore, and clearly no chance of me ever getting back together with her, this stroke of luck could have not come for me at a better time.

Like my first girlfriend, she was another one of the real stunners from the neighborhood that I knew was way out of my league. So as happy as I was to hear the news, I could not help but wonder what she could have possibly wanted with a pimpled face character like me. Pimples notwithstanding, I didn't ask any questions, and got right down to the business at hand. She lived at the top of LaSalle St. and in one of the buildings of our housing complex. The truth of the matter is that I'd had my eyes on her for some time. But because my chances with her seemed so unlikely, I always treaded lightly around her. That being said, realizing that my chances were better than I thought, I seized the moment without the slightest hesitation. Feeling more experienced this time around, I gave it another try by popping "the question" again; and when she told me, yes, I was happy to know that I had a girlfriend again.

She is a nice person; and she was fun, easy going, and easy to get along with. She was also unique, interesting, and kind of quiet; and these things made her that much more mysterious and appealing to me. She was a Puerto Rican girl; and being fluent in Spanish, she helped me with my Spanish whenever I had a question about something. I felt pretty lucky because I knew that I had a pretty unique and interesting person for a girlfriend.

At about this time, while playing basketball at Stone Gym one evening, a kid recovered a loose ball under the basket. He was crouched down and bent over to protect the ball from me while deciding what he was going to do next. I stood over him with my arms and hands stretched out to prevent him from scoring. Then, suddenly, he leaped up to score a quick basket, trying to catch me by surprise. He did indeed catch me by surprise, because his clean-shaved head slammed right into my lower lip. The force of the blow knocked me back several feet and down onto the floor. When I recovered from the shock of being hit so hard, I realized that my lip was cut and bleeding badly. I cupped my hand under my chin and went to the bathroom to see the extent of my injury. After seeing the damage, I realized that my two front teeth had cut my lower lip. Then, along with the cut on the inside of my lip, the skin was broken just below the outside of my lower lip too. Clearly, basketball was over for me for the night, and I hurried home so my mother could take me to the emergency room. The doctor gave me three stitches on the inside of my lip and sent me home.

When I checked my injury the next morning, I noticed that my lip was slightly swollen. Since it seemed normal that some swelling would come from such a bad cut, I didn't think much of it. But by the next day, my bottom lip had swollen to twice its normal size. So now, along with my pimples, I had a very fat bottom lip, too. I was some kind of sight to see, and it was not exactly the look I wanted, being a slightly shy teenager, with a new girlfriend. If fat lips were the fashion statement then that they have become more recently, it might have not been so bad; a collagen injection would have not come close to doing the (not so attractive) lip enhancement job that my injury did for my lower lip. So in the middle of my summer vacation, I was in seclusion, and I wouldn't even walk 60 feet down the hallway to throw out the garbage for fear of being seen. When my friends came to visit me, I swore them to secrecy, and I got their word (I think) to say nothing about my hideously swollen lip to anyone, including my girlfriend.

Given my injury's turn for the worse, my mother took me back to the emergency room. After filling the doctor in on the details of my injury and treatment, he was surprised and critical of the shabby care that I had been given. Much to his credit and given his very good bedside manner, he didn't laugh once when he saw how fat my lip was. Instead, he told me that the previous doctor should have cleaned out the wound and given me a prescription for antibiotics to prevent it from becoming infected. He told me, too, that by not cleaning out the cut and only stitching it up, he had, essentially, closed the germs (from my mouth) inside the wound. After this very conscientious doctor explained all of this to me, he took the stitches out, gave me a prescription for antibiotics, and told me to soak my lip with a clean face cloth dipped in warm salt water. I followed his instructions, and much to my relief my fat lip shrank down to its normal size in a day or two. I still had my pimples, but my fat lip was finally gone.

With my injury costing me a week of my precious summer vacation, I was eager to get back outside. Even more than that, I wanted to get back up the street to see my girlfriend again. We stayed together for a little longer, but it came to an end in pretty much the same way it did with my first girlfriend. A mutual friend called me to the side one day to tell me the news. She told me that she had been asked to tell me that it was over between my girlfriend and me. Interestingly enough, this intermediary's name is Carol. I mentioned her earlier, and I mentioned that she is Dizzy Gillespie's niece. So despite this unfortunate turn of events for me, I can at least say that I have the distinction of saying that Dizzy Gillespie's niece is the one who brought me the news. Not only that, but I can say that I had a pretty unique and interesting girlfriend. So in the end, knowing that there was nothing that I could do about it, clearly it was time for me to move on to my next high school and teenage adventure in Morningside Heights.

6

Our Name Was
Orchestra Flamboyan

B y way of a popular NYC disc jockey, Latin music's remarkable surge continued. To everyone he was known as Symphony Sid (or just "Sid"), and he enthusiastically promoted the music and dance scene by providing his listeners with the excellent Latin dance music being played in NYC clubs during that time. So on Thursday, Friday, and Saturday nights, his show was a virtual radio town hall meeting on Latin music. Anything we wanted to know about bands, albums, where bands were playing, and who was who on the scene, it was all at the dials of our radios, via the Symphony Sid Show.

Eddy Zervigon, Johnny Pacheco, Eddie Palmieri, Mongo Santamaria, Ray Barretto, Jose Fajardo, Joe Cuba, La Lupe, Willie Bobo, Orlando Marin, Machito, Lou Perez, Tito Puente, Joe Quijano, Ricardo Ray, Pete Rodriguez, Celia Cruz, Charlie Palmieri, and Tito Rodriguez (all with their very distinct styles of music) set the stage for a Latin music scene that was, without question, New York City's golden age of salsa.

As captivated as I was by it all, along with wanting a Cuban flute, another dream of mine was to put a Latin band together. As much as I enjoyed listening and dancing, neither seemed to do enough for me; so I had a clear sense that I needed more. Then when I learned that musicians were paid to play, I was sure that I had to become involved from the musician's side of things. So two friends of mine and I decided to make this dream of ours come true. One of my friends' name is Kenneth Miller. He was with me when we both thought the tugboat on the Hudson River was going to break into a highly amplified version of the song, "El Watusi." We'd been classmates since the fourth grade, and he was at the Americana Hotel when Johnny Pacheco blew the roof off the place. While I watched Johnny Pacheco that night, Kenneth must have had his eyes on what the timbale player was doing, given his preference for timbales.

My other friend, Gregory Cooper, was a year younger than Kenneth and me, but he had a head start on both of us. His older brother learned to play congas with a group of Cuban or Puerto Rican drummers in their old neighborhood; and he taught Gregory when Gregory was 8 years old. Then Gregory taught me. Gregory was with me when Eddie Palmieri and his band opened up their show at the Apollo Theater in the memorable way that they did. Gregory is very funny; and, to this day, I am convinced that he could have easily been a very good standup comedian if he'd chosen to take that career path. As much as he has always loved playing conga drums, he didn't like carrying them. So I kept his drums at my house and carried them to our rehearsals for him. This gave me a chance to practice all the things he taught me about playing them. Both Kenneth and Gregory are very fun, funny, intelligent, and interesting guys with very good ears for music. The three of us could dissect and analyze the layers and facets of this music for hours on end, and always find something new and interesting to point out to each other about it as we listened.

Benjamin (Tito) Marrero and his younger brother Ricardo (Richie) lived in Kenneth's building, and they already had a band. They rehearsed in Grant's community center right behind my building. I earlier mentioned that Richie went on to play with Ruben Blades and his group, "Seis del Solar." On warm summer nights, I used to stretch out on my bed and listen to Tito, Richie, and their band as the music wafted straight up and into my bedroom window. Hearing the cowbells, conga drums, claves, maracas, guiro, bongos, timbales, and horns was a real treat for me. Then too, I used to go to watch them rehearse at J.H.S. 43, and watching them made me want to play Latin music even more.

On the day Kenneth brought his new set of timbales home, it felt like a big step forward for us. Then it wasn't long before he was able to play the bell patterns, rim shots, abanicos (fans), licks, and fills that timbale players have to know, to play Latin music. Being able to see so many outstanding timbale players, Kenneth became an excellent drummer in no time. In his room, I watched him as he placed, positioned, and tightened his drumheads and cowbell clamps for the first time. Then before I knew it, he played as if he'd been playing for years. With Gregory playing congas since he was eight, there was not much for him to do, other than wait for Kenneth and me to bring our playing up to speed. Given all that Gregory had to offer, we were lucky to have him as a close friend and as a part of our musical adventure.

As the band's flute player, I had to do my part too if I were not going to hinder the big plans we had for ourselves. I had to watch, listen, learn, and practice. Not only did I have to learn as much as I could about the technical side of flute playing, but I had to learn the unique, percussive, syncopated, rhythmic, and improvisational flute playing style used in Cuban music. Pacheco and all of the other flute players made it look easy, but as I soon realized, it was going to take much more work than I thought. It is a unique flute playing style with a vocabulary, accent, swing, and language of its own; Cuban musicians call it playing with (or in) clave. Additionally, a Cuban styled flute player has to have a good imagination, as well as a collection of accessible riffs and phrases at the top of his or her head to avoid being repetitive while improvising. Fortunately for me, the flute was very popular in Latin music at that time, so there were more than enough flute players for me to listen to, watch, and learn from. Of course, there was Johnny Pacheco, Jorge Castro, Joe Canura, and Lou Perez, but with the recent arrival of Jose Fajardo and Eddy Zervigon from Cuba, I had two additional five-key flute players to learn from too.

As I mentioned, unbeknownst to me, Eddy Zervigon lived only ten blocks from me (on 135th Street and right off Broadway). This was where he formed and rehearsed with his band, Orquesta Broadway, and they rehearsed at his first floor apartment. Living there, forming his band there, and rehearsing there too was how the band's name was chosen. Much to the credit and hard work of Eddy Zervigon, Orquesta Broadway is a band that was formed only ten short blocks from my neighborhood in 1962, still plays presently, and is known and loved around the world. As taken as I was by the NYC Latin music scene, it would have been some kind of thrill for me to see Eddy in the neighborhood during that time or to accidentally stumble upon one of their rehearsals up on 135th Street.

I could tell that Maria, the owner of our popular neighborhood pizzeria, was at a loss to understand why an English-speaking African-American kid played Eddy Zervigon's hit tune, Mi Socio, as much as I did on her jukebox whenever I came in for a slice of pizza and a soda. It was the only song I played, and I played it two or three times while there. His flute playing, and my slice of pizza and soda were perfect treats for my taste buds and eardrums.

As I mentioned, Jorge Castro was another excellent flute player on the NYC Latin music scene during that time, and I saw him play a lot. He played with Eddie Palmieri and his band, Conjunto La Perfecta. Jorge Castro is Puerto Rican, but he played the wooden five-key Cuban flute. Additionally, Joe Canura was another very good flute player. He played with Ray Barretto's band, La Moderna, and he played the Boehm silver flute. Then there was Lou Perez. He was a piano player, but as I found out later, he was a flute player too. I do not know where Julio Guerrero lived, but he played flute on a popular recording that was out during that time called The Cuban Jam Session. I do not know where Rolando Lozano lived either, but he played flute with Mongo Santamaria. Julio Guerrero and Rolando Lozano are both Cuban and were two additional five-key flute players that I listened to.

I had the recordings of all of these fine flute players, and I was always on the lookout for new five-key flute players to listen to. I studied them all closely and made every effort to capture, internalize, and recreate that rich Cuban sound and feeling. When I went to see them play, they were always helpful; and if they were playing from written music, they were always good about letting me see what their music looked like, written out on paper.

Along with bringing my flute playing up to speed, I had to learn how to write out musical arrangements too. In our effort to determine the sound and style we wanted for the band, we experimented with trombones, saxophones, and trumpets. Since these instruments are tuned differently and require different key signatures, knowing how to write music for each one is essential. Then just as well, I had to learn the details for writing the music for piano and bass for Latin music too. So, for me, this was a real crash course in music theory and music writing rolled into one. It was a good thing that my mother had a piano. Having such easy access to it, I was able to write out the piano, flute, and bass music, and add the melodies and harmonies for the horns we used.

When our first piano player didn't work out, right in Kenneth's building was a piano player named Ellsworth Edenfield. Like the rest of us, Ellsworth had never played Latin music, but he had a very natural touch for piano playing. He played for his mother's church; and he liked playing for fun. He enjoyed playing oldies, doo-wap, and boogie-woogie music too. Not only did he have a natural touch for piano playing, but he also had a memory like a steel trap. He did not read music at all, but if we showed him how to play something one time, he picked it up quickly, remembered it, and played it back perfectly with every bit of the flavor and feeling of Latin music. Not only that, but somehow, he already knew how to improvise in the Latin music piano-playing style too. Then, in a surprisingly impressive way, the more he played, the better he got at it. So we were lucky to have another close friend from the neighborhood who was right onboard with the rest of us in heart, soul, mind, and spirit. He was fun, funny, enthusiastic, talented, and a ham of sorts. So fortunately for us, right in three buildings of our nine-building housing complex, there were four of us who were motivated, loved Latin music, loved rehearsing, laughing, joking, and spending time together. By our names we sounded like a jazz quartet rather than a Latin band, but we had not even slightest doubt or hesitance about making this unusual leap into a style of music that was so new to us. We were the rock-solid foundation of NYC's Orchestra Flamboyan. So now with this foundation in place, we still needed to find a bass player, a horn section, and a singer to complete our ensemble.

Fate and much luck continued to work in our favor; one of Tito Marrero's singers approached us about joining our band. After hearing us, he must have seen or heard something that he liked, because he left Tito's much more developed band to sing with us. Fortunately Tito had another singer, so he was not left high and dry without a singer. We were pretty close with the Marrero family (and, very often, we got together and played music at their house), so I did not want Tito or Richie to think that we were trying to fatten up our band by stealing their musicians. So I told Tito that Frankie approached us. Very humorously, he told me that he'd been trying to get rid of Frankie for some time, and then he thanked me for helping him get Frankie off his hands. I do not know if this were true or not, but Frankie joining us had no negative impact on our good connection and friendship with Tito or Richie, they remained as supportive of us as always. Frankie's birth name was Frankie Cerda, and eventually he changed it to Frankie Dante, a stage name that he preferred. Like Ellsworth, Frankie was another character. Additionally, Frankie was so fun loving and enthusiastic about playing music that he was a perfect match for us.

Frankie was born in the Dominican Republic; so having him in the band solved several problems for us. Fluent in Spanish, he provided us with better lyrics and choruses for our songs. Then too, hanging out with him over the years, did wonders for my Spanish-speaking and comprehension. Though he lived on East 34th Street, the distance between our two neighborhoods was not a problem for him at all. He was just as eager to rehearse and play as we were. So with his small tote bag that he proudly carried his guiro and maracas in, and a pair of feet that turned out to almost a full 180 degrees, he was at every rehearsal on time and ready to get down to the business of making music.

Frankie was the one who came up with the name for our band, Orchestra Flamboyan. If you were a part of the NYC Latin music scene during the mid 60s, the chances are good that you know who we were, seen us play, or even danced at one or more of our performances. We played all over the city. In the movie El Cantante depicting the life of singer Hector Lavoe (by Jennifer Lopez and Marc Anthony), our band's name appears on a flyer that spins out and onto the middle of the screen. It is the original flyer that was used to advertise a boat ride we played with Willie Colon, his band, and his legendary singer, Hector Lavoe. When I asked Frankie about the name, he told me that "flamboyan" is the name of a tree that grows in Puerto Rico and Cuba. We all liked the idea, so Orchestra Flamboyan was the name of the band from that point on.

After toiling with several bass players, we found a very good one who lived a few blocks up Amsterdam Avenue in the Manhattanville Housing Projects. His name is Eddie Gonzales. His father was a professional bass player who played with the house band at the Roseland Ballroom in Midtown, and Eddie Jr. was a chip off the old block. Though Eddie Jr. was an outstanding bass player and was exactly what we needed, I cannot say he was the most reliable musician I'd ever had the pleasure of playing music with. Knowing how much we depended on him, he had a knack for being a no show for gigs from time to time. He was our first experience with a flaky musician. Being so new at this, for the life of me, I could not understand the thinking of a musician like that. I thought all musicians were just as enthusiastic, thrilled, and eager to play and rehearse as I was. Despite having a bass player who we could not always count on, we were lucky enough to have another solid bass player named Eddie Reyes who lived in Manhattanville too. He was very good and very reliable. He was a big guy, too; and everyone called him "Buff." Buff was short for Buffalo, two nicknames that our fun, good-natured, and excellent bass player was tagged with.

As impossible as it is to capture the true sound and feeling of this music without a bass, whenever Eddie Gonzales was a no show for any of our performances, remarkably, people would still tell us how much they liked us, or asked for a phone number to reach us for an event they were planning. Then when Eddie did grace us with his presence, or if Buff substituted, we really gave everyone their money's worth.

Everyone from the neighborhood knew about us, and they gave us a lot of support for our effort, determination, and accomplishments. We pushed far into New York City's outstanding Latin music scene, and given the many bands that were out and playing at the time, this was a considerable accomplishment for us.

After experimenting with different horn combinations, we settled on using two trombones. This style was relatively new and different; and it was made popular by Eddie Palmieri. Our good fortune continued when I enlisted the services of two trombone players from Spanish Harlem, Angelo Rodriguez and Chickie Fuentes. They were a couple of fun-loving guys, too, who absolutely loved playing music. Angelo played with Johnny

Colon and Chickie played with Joe Bataan. They both gave it their all each and every time. Percussionist Milton Cardona, played with us too at a point in the process, and so did Chucky Lopez (Tommy Lopez's son).

Having so much to do, we spent much of our time rehearsing. As much as we loved getting together to rehearse, it took practically no effort to round everyone up. Having a piano in my living room, and with my mother's consent, support, blessings, and love for music, our first few rehearsals were right in her living room.

Incidentally and interestingly enough, at one of our rehearsals at a nightclub in Harlem called the Devil's Inn, we noticed a guy standing in the doorway looking in, and listening to us play. After getting a better look, we realized that it was Kareem Abdul-Jabbar. He came in and sat down to listen and talk with us. He appeared to have taken an interest in us, and what we were doing; and he appeared to take a particular interest and liking to my unique Boehm-styled wooden flute. He asked me if he could see it, took it into his hands, and then he played it. After talking with us, he was soon up and on his way. From time to time, I wonder if he remembers our brief but enjoyable encounter; I know, for sure that I never forgot it; it was a special moment for me, and the other band members too.

So if we were not rehearsing, some combination of Gregory, Kenneth, Frankie, Ellsworth, and I would get together to go to see the heavy hitters in action, take mental notes, and then talk about it enthusiastically on the way home and the next day. Without question, the most popular music and dance venue for Latin music was a place in Midtown called the Palladium. For a $1.50 cover charge, and a twenty-minute (15-cents) train ride, we were able to see just about any band we wanted. Manhattan Center was another very large venue in Midtown that promoters used for big and special events. Other popular NYC venues for Latin music at that time were the Bronx Music Palace, the Village Gate, Hunts Point Palace, the Corso, the Round Table, the Palm Garden, the Club Cabo Rojeño, the Red Garter, Riverside Plaza, the Havana-San Juan, the Colegate Gardens, the Club Three-&-One, and the Cheetah. There were also summer concerts at night in Central Park and boat rides with bands playing as people danced while cruising around Manhattan. There were several after-hours clubs in

Spanish Harlem and the Havana-San Juan was just north of Morningside Heights. Without a doubt, this was NYC's golden age of salsa. I say this, not only because of the outstanding bands, music, dancing, clubs, and eclectic Latin musical styles being played, but also because of the wide assortment of people that the music was starting to attract.

Creative promoters, like Ralph Mercado, came up with all kinds of interesting ways to bring this fabulous music to the dancing public, and the bands never let the dancing public down. The dancers responded in kind by flocking to these dances and events in droves. So by tuning in to the Symphony Sid Show or seeing one of the flyers advertising the various events posted up at train station entrances, in record stores, and on billboards, as budding musicians, we knew right where to go for shots of inspiration and regular updates to our rich education on the fine art of playing African-based Latin music.

7

Fun City, Summertime, & the Golden Age of Salsa

For two of my high school summer vacations, I was hired for my second job as a counselor for children. The Lenox Hill Day Camp was my employer this time, and like my first job, it was an excellent experience having the safety and wellbeing of so many children in our hands. The director divided us into several groups and allowed us to budget and plan our daily activities. Riding the hot and crowded subway trains as much as we did, there was no room for error. So we worked closely as a counseling team holding train doors open and counting heads to be sure we returned with each and every child.

On one fun outing, we took the kids up to the Apollo Theater to see the Temptations. We went to an afternoon performance, and because we had children with us, the price for admission was cut in half. It seemed to me that it would be a fun, new, and different adventure for our twenty, or so, lap-of-luxury kids from the east side of Manhattan who had never heard of Harlem, the Temptations, or the Apollo Theater. Along with that, it gave us counselors a chance to see the Temptations with Lenox Hill picking up the tab. To my surprise, the theater was empty when we arrived; so we took front row seats. It was the middle of the week, and since most people went at night and on the weekend, we were the only ones there. As a result, we were given a private, close up, and personal performance by the world-renowned Temptations. The kids loved it; and despite playing for such a small audience, the Temptations turned in a spectacular performance. I knew that my idea went over well with our young clients because they talked about it, excitedly, all the way back to Lenox Hill.

I cannot say enough about how good it was for me to grow up in New York City during that time. It was such a great place to live during the early, mid, and late sixties. Though much like today, we were promised everything under the sun by many of the self-serving public servants, words like inflation, debt ceilings, recession, voter fraud, fiscal cliffs, homelessness, sequesters, government shutdowns, partisanship, and budget deficits were never heard. Compared to now, the cost of living was low and there was work for everyone; then along with that, the overwhelming majority of our public servants were more concerned about the well being of the people they were there to serve. We indeed had our problems at that time, but the human flaws and foibles we lived with took very little from living in what was commonly called Fun City. The power outage of 1965 that plunged the entire city into darkness while I sat in my living room doing homework, the "Mad Bomber's" reign of terror, the muggings, and the train door operators who joyfully made a sporting event of closing train doors on people as they ran to catch the train were all a part of living in "Fun City." Rogue drivers intentionally splashed puddles of rainwater or slush from melted snow on people who innocently waited to cross the street. These were only a few of the things that we had to endure. In spite of it all, I would have not traded Morningside Heights, Harlem, or Fun City in for any other place in the world (including Hawaii where I spent a lot of time during my early teenage years [in many of my vivid, extravagant, and far-reaching daydreams]).

While starting to appreciate how privileged I was to live in such a vibrant, cultural, and diverse neighborhood and city, like a bolt out of the blue, my mother told me that she was thinking about packing everything up and moving the family to South Carolina. I don't remember what I said when the full impact of her words hit me between the eyes a second or two later. I can only say that they were not words of support for the idea. It had been a good ten years since I'd been to South Carolina, and with the niche and lifestyle that I had carved out for myself, the idea of moving away from it all was hardly something that I wanted to hear or talk about. I knew that it would be impossible for me to replace the things I enjoyed in NYC, in South Carolina.

As my mother and I argued the pros and cons of moving, the fits and tantrums I threw were not small or pretty, nor would they dignify anyone my age at that time. Thinking about this now, I understand why my parents didn't tell me about their plan to move from Hamilton Heights. The mere talk of moving from NYC brought a dramatic performance from me that I didn't even know I was capable of. As a big, but empty bluff, and having no idea of how I could have done it, I told my mother that I was not going to leave if she decided to move. Since I melted down, completely, whenever she tried to talk to me about it, she thought that it would be better to postpone the discussions to give the idea a little time to sink in. Trying to talk to me about moving was like throwing gasoline on a fire. I was a pretty laid-back and easy-going kid, but I had a very short fuse when it came to trying to talk to me about moving. I never knew how my sister or brother felt about it, but the thought of moving traumatized me and practically made me physically ill. As much as I complained, it was good that I, at least, had some forewarning this time.

With plenty of reasons for my resistance, two in particular might help to see why my reaction to moving was so extreme: One day I went to Tito and Richie Marrero's house for a visit. After getting there, Richie had some news for me that just about knocked me off my feet. He told me that Johnny Pacheco had just left, and I had just missed getting a chance to meet him by only a few minutes. He was surprised that I didn't see him in the hallway on my way in, and he mentioned that I was very likely riding up on one elevator while Pacheco was on his way down on the other one. By that time, the entire neighborhood knew of the big Johnny Pacheco fan I was. As disappointing as it was for me to have missed seeing him, it was still exciting for me to know that he had been to our neighborhood. As it turned out, Tito and Richie's sister knew one of Pacheco's singers, and Pacheco happened to be with him during his visit with her that day.

Then too, soon after, something similar happened in my building. While on my way home, I stepped into the elevator. After pressing the button for my floor, I saw a guy who looked familiar to me. Actually, I knew who he was right away, but seeing him on the elevator in my building was so out of the ordinary that it took several seconds for me to get it all into some kind of logical order in my head. When I did, I realized that I had it right. The guy was Pete "El Conde" Rodriguez. Pete Rodriguez was not only Johnny Pacheco's most popular singer, but he was Pacheco's best friend. Additionally, pound for pound, he was one of the best, beloved, and popular singers to come out of the NYC Latin music scene during that time.

There were six or seven other people in the elevator, including the woman that Pete was with. During the short ride, he didn't notice me, and I was so surprised by seeing him that I didn't say anything to him. The elevator reached my floor before I knew it, and I got off and walked to my apartment, disappointed at myself for not saying anything to him when I had such a good opportunity to. As disappointed as I was, it worked out even better for me, because it gave me an idea. At home I went right to my record collection and pulled out a stack of my Pacheco albums (most of which Pete "El Conde" sang on). Then very carefully, I placed "Pacheco at The New York Worlds Fair" at the very top and "Viva Africa" right under it. Then I put Suavito, Cañonazo, and five or six other Pacheco albums with them. Tucked under my arm, and quite visible, I bolted out the door and down the hall. Much satisfied with myself for coming up with this idea, I smiled while thinking about it as I waited for the elevator. If there were a better way for me to meet and talk to "Pete El Conde" other than casually bumping into him while "coincidentally" carrying a stack of Pacheco albums, I do not know what it could have been.

After a few anxious minutes waiting for the elevator (and hoping that he had not already left the building), the elevator finally came. I opened the door and stepped inside. The elevator appeared to be empty, but after stepping inside, in the right-hand corner of the elevator, I saw Pete "El

Conde," standing there by himself, and no one else was in the elevator; so it was only Pete and me, face to face.. I didn't expect my plan to take this sudden turn, and I started to feel a little nervous and self-conscious about my wacky plan. My heart started to race, skip, and thump as I felt beads of sweat starting to collect at the pores of my forehead. Then right before a torrential downpour of flop sweat embarrassed me, I saw that he noticed my stack of albums. After seeing them, he smiled and was so friendly that I was quickly able to regain my composure. The woman with him was still at her relatives' apartment, and Pete was on his way downstairs to wait for her in front of the building. So I ended up talking with him for about thirty minutes. Along with telling him of the big Pacheco fan I am, I told him that I was a flute player. We talked until his girlfriend came downstairs. He introduced me to her, and the three of us talked for a short while before they left. Subsequently, I saw them entering or leaving the building three or four other times, and I got to know them pretty well. So, from that point on, whenever he saw me at any of his performances with Pacheco, he always made it a point to come over to say hello to me. This impressed and caught more than just one or two of my friends by surprise.

I saw the great Cuban singer, La Lupe, in our neighborhood too, just as she came out of the popular Cotton Club on W. 125th Street just as I walked by the front door with a small group of friends. Along with that, my longtime friend and band mate, Kenneth Miller, told me recently that he used to see her in the neighborhood quite often. There was a small but growing Dominican/Cuban community just north of Morningside Heights; as I mentioned, Eddy Zervigon lived in that area, and a club called the Havana-San Juan was there too. I even caught one of Johnny Pacheco's performances at the Havana-San Juan. So along with everything else, our neighborhood was proving itself to be a small, but interesting hub of activity for Latin music, too. With our neighborhood and NYC making these kinds of things possible, the many places to hear music, our band coming together nicely, good summer jobs, my love for Latin music being what it was, and so many other things to keep me busy, the idea of moving away from it all was a big concern for me.

The Palladium was New York City's hallmark of Latin music dance venues. All of the clubs were good, but none really filled the void the Palladium left when it closed unexpectedly during the mid-60s. Since the Palladium Ballroom was open every weekend, if there were bands that I wanted to see, it would not be long before they would be making an appearance there. It was on Broadway and just off 53rd Street. A twenty-minute train ride from 125th Street seemed to get us there in no time. So in NYC's summer heat, humidity, rain, hail, sleet, or snow, my friends, band members, and I would usually be the first ones to arrive, with me leading the charge. The dance floor was buffed, waxed, and spruced up nicely before each show; and I'd arrived there so early one time, the buffing machine was still in the middle of the dance floor.

Though the ballroom was a good size, it barely held the many people who came to dance and enjoy the music. But what made it extra special was that it was small enough to allow for a perfect connection between the bands and dancers. Along with that, the Palladium provided my friends and me with an escape for music and dancing every weekend. We stood at the front of the stage so much that the musicians practically knew us, and they were always good about chatting with us too. The front half of the stage was about a foot high, and the back half of the stage was a foot or two higher; so we were able to watch the bands play from only a few feet away, and at almost eye level. The ballroom's acoustics caught, absorbed, and dispersed the music perfectly.

We paid for our tickets at a street level ticket booth just inside the front door; and the ballroom was at the top of a flight of stairs. There were seats and booths with tables along the walls, and a foot high fencelike enclosure circled the hardwood dance floor. Four or five breaks in the partition gave the dancers quick and easy access to the dance floor at the start of each song. There was one microphone at the front and center of the stage for the singers, and another microphone (with a cloth wrapped around it) was stuffed into the soundboard of a baby grand piano. This made it possible to hear the piano and the singers very well. It was very low-tech sound engineering by today's standards, but it got the job done quite well. The flute players played acoustically, or used the singer's microphone for their solos. These days, each instrument is played into a microphone, and passed through an elaborate sound system.

If I were not dancing or watching the bands at the front of the stage, I would stand at the right/rear side of the stage, behind the piano players. From there, not only was I able to watch the skillful keyboard players up closely, but sometimes, I was able to see how the "piano charts" for Latin music are written. Then, whenever Eddie Palmieri or Ricardo Ray played (the two top compelling band leading pianists), I spent plenty of time in that small area.

The Sunday night Palladium crowd was made up of African-American high school teenagers; and our unrestrained passion for Latin music and dancing was such that the ballroom was always packed to capacity (and beyond) for these Sunday night dances. Though I usually went on Sunday nights, if there were bands that I wanted to see on Friday or Saturday nights, I went on those nights too. The owner of the Palladium was a guy named Max Hyman, and the manager was a guy named Catalino Rolon, and if there were any flaws in the Palladium's operation, I cannot tell you what they were. It was first class in every way, and they met the dancing needs of a cross-section of people like no other NYC Latin dance venue; so for that reason, there were never any slow nights at the Palladium. New York City's most popular Latin dance venue opened its doors for the first time in 1948, so by the time I started to go, they had long honed their operation to pure perfection.

The Palladium became a venue for Latin music in an interesting way. Before it became the Palladium, as we knew it, the beautiful ballroom was once an exclusive dance studio for various types of ballroom dancing. Then when it started to lose money due to a regular low turnout, the owner came close to closing it down. But before this happened, Federico Pagani, a Latin music promoter approached the owner and suggested they try their hand at Latin music since it had been doing so well in Spanish Harlem and in the Bronx; then the rest was history.

When I learned to dance, Latin music had just undergone a significant change. More and more, smaller bands started to emerge and fill the ranks of the Benny Moré, Dezi Arnez-type big-band orchestras of the fifties. This was a pivotal time for Latin music in NYC, and the Palladium presented these larger bands on Friday and Saturday nights catering to an older generation of "Anglo" and Spanish-speaking dancers. On either one of these nights, big bands like Tito Puente, Tito Rodriguez, Machito, El Gran Combo, or La Sonora Matancera played. But the Palladium's management team knew all too well how much we African-American kids loved these new, smaller, eight piece powerhouse bands, and they would usually always have them on the bill for the Sunday night dances. This new wave of bands led by Johnny Pacheco, Eddie Palmieri, Ray Barretto, Eddy Zervigon, Joe Cuba, Ricardo Ray, and Pete (Boogaloo) Rodriguez played for these Sunday night dances, and they were, virtually, musical flamethrowers who regularly lit fires under the feet of dancers each and every time they took the stage. Cutting-edge, spellbinding pianist, bandleader, composer, and arranger Ricardo Ray had a song called, Echando Candela, (or in English: Throwing Fire). It is a pretty hard driving, high voltage tune about what they do night after night for the (female) dancers that came to hear them play. Given the high quality of NYC's Latin music scene at that time, for all intent and purposes, Richie Ray and his singers could have been singing about all of the other bands, too, and what they all did for the dancers (male and female) from that era. The music from this group of musicians is timeless; and listening to it now (more that 50 years later) takes me back to our living room where I spent countless listening hours. Time has not diminished the music's brilliance; and it still gives me goose bumps. And now that my Spanish is much better than it was back then, this adds a whole new exciting element to listening to it now, that I could not fully appreciate before.

Very often I got there before the bands, and it was fun for me to watch these larger than life musicians arrive by taxicab to unload their equipment before going inside. It was like watching star athletes arrive to a stadium before a game. From start to finish, a level of energy was generated in the Palladium Ballroom that almost defied description. The first set was a taste of things to come for the rest of the night. After a full set's worth of gaining traction, the bands dug in even more during the second set and went right for the ears, hearts, and feet of the dancers. Then for a finale, the third set was like a parting shot that gave everyone plenty to think about, that added an extra bounce to their step on the way home.

The bands never overloaded the dancers by going from one song to the next in rapid-fire succession. Instead, between each song, they took a minute or two before starting the next one. Not only did this create an element of anticipation and surprise, but it gave the male dancers plenty of time to find and position themselves close to the next person they wanted to dance with. As we guys jockeyed for position, it was like getting into position for a rebound on a basketball court. No elbows were thrown, but there were plenty of screens being set, and a lot of blocking out. Then when the band started to play, a circle of hands would shoot out quickly at women, in every part of the ballroom, asking them to dance; then from these groups of guys the women would choose.

It was some kind of place for music and dancing. With the outstanding music being what it was, the dancers had a pretty spectacular show of their own going on in the middle of the dance floor. The dancing was so good that we were able to dance without bumping into each other or stepping on each other's feet in such close quarters. Very often a dancing couple would heat up and catch everyone's attention. When this happened, all of the other dancers would stop dancing, clear out a space for them, and form a circle around the dancing pair to watch and cheer them on. We called this, "pulling a ring." Sometimes, people brought whistles and blew them loudly to show their approval whenever the music hit the top of a fevered pitch. This had a way of ratcheting the energy levels up even more; so these Sunday night dances at the Palladium were like revival meetings.

Since the dancers could have easily danced until daybreak, the Palladium had a nice way of letting everyone know when the last song was being played. Near the end of the last song, and right when the music, the band, and the dancing had long entered the upper stratosphere, they would start to flick the lights off and on, as the dancers made every effort to squeeze the last few drops of pleasure from the Palladium experience for the night. Along with letting people know that it was the last song, it also provided a bit of a special effect that nicely rapped up the music and dancing for the evening. It appeared as if the intensity of the music and the dancing were jarring the building's electrical system. Then even with the flickering lights, it still took some time to get everyone out of the building, as people stood around stunned, spent, euphoric, and clearly not quite ready to leave.

This light flickering was dramatic, and it was something to see when Eddie Palmieri closed out his Sunday night performances at the Palladium with his epic hit tune, Azucar Pa' Ti (Sugar for You). It was perhaps Eddie Palmieri's biggest hit, and he saved it for the last song of the night after skillfully building the intensity by bombarding us with one hit tune after the other, Tu Tu Ta Ta, Café, Descarga Palmieri, Oyelo Que Te Conviene, Mi Sonsito, Quidate Compay, Sin Sabor Nada, Bon-Boncito de Pozo, and too many more to include. Azucar Pa' Ti was the perfect song to end the night with; being the scorcher of a tune that it is, it never failed to push the music and dancing completely over the edge.

So whenever we heard Azucar's more than familiar opening refrain, there would be a mad scramble for us guys to find our favorite dancers. After that, and well into the song, as Eddie came out of his mesmerizing 5, 8, and sometimes 10 minute piano solos, sweat would be pouring from his face and head. During his piano solos in Azucar Pa' Ti, he improvised with his right hand while holding down a steady montuno pattern with his left hand; it was pretty astounding to see and hear someone do something like that. It were as if he had two brains working on it, or as if two people were at the piano playing. Throughout the piano solo and the song, Eddie would growl in an audible buzz like purr (due to the pleasure that he gets from playing). At the end of his piano solo, Eddie's bass player and conga player (Dave Perez and Tommy Lopez) would go into a highly charged alternating Afro-Cuban rhythmic pattern, called guaguanco. Right behind this shift in the music, Manny Oquendo would switch back to playing the (louder) cowbell after playing the (more quiet) shells (or sides) of the timbales during Eddie's piano solo. Combined, these changes in the music seemed to send a charge of electricity throughout the ballroom that was a clear indicator to all that there would be more to come, and that both Eddie Palmieri and his band were not quite finished with us just yet. Perfectly coordinated with the music at this point, they started to flick the lights off and on. This confluence of events pushed the highly charged music and dancing to another level, and Jorge Castro would then step to the microphone to get his flute solo started. While this was happening, Barry Rogers and Jose Rodriguez (Eddie's two trombone players) would stand with their trombones slung over their forearms as they took everything in contemplatively, and waited for their time to join in on the action again. With Eddie almost completely drenched in sweat and his eyes focused in on nothing in particular, it seemed as if he had slipped into another world. Meanwhile, if an idea came to Barry Rogers for a new, different, or interesting trombone line to back Jorge Castro up with, he would lean over and play it softly one time for Jose to hear, and Jose would nod his head. Then, soon after, when the two trombones joined in, they added a one-two punch that slowly built in volume and intensity; and before long we all knew that Eddie Palmieri and his Conjunto La Prefecta had unleashed a tidal wave of sound to end the night of dancing with.

Perfectly coordinated with the flickering lights, everything was sent into overdrive, and by that time, Eddie had taken us into this other world too. Most people danced, but many others stood at the front of the stage to watch the band, spellbound and awestruck; sometimes it seemed as if the entire building were swaying along with the music. During these special moments, my (very funny) friend and band mate, Gregory Cooper (who is never at a loss for words) used to say to me, "Eddie's gone!" Knowing very little or no Spanish, many of the African-American teenagers did their best to join in with the singing. Instead of singing "Azucar," Gregory and I saw a girl singing "bazooka" instead. Though we laughed about it, we both knew that she was feeling the music as much as everyone else.

When the music ended for the night, the sharply dressed dancers would be drenched in sweat, with handkerchiefs hanging around their necks or mopping their brows with them. Though soaked, we would be exhilarated from the experience at the end of the night. So the Palladium was not only a perfect escape for music and dancing, but it was another one of many schools that gave us a chance to see and learn how this music is played and presented.

Playing the modern Boehm silver flute for my high school orchestra was another priceless lesson for me about playing and presenting music. We played classical music and the experience filled in a lot of what I missed by learning to play without a flute teacher. Our musical director, Mr. Klinger, and a coterie of fine musicians made it possible for me to be a part of an exceptional musical experience.

At the end of the school year we played a series of spring concerts for the tenth, eleventh, and twelfth grade classes. Then, we played an evening concert for the entire school, parents, and other invited guests. I played in these spring concerts while in the eleventh and twelfth grades. We practiced all year for these four performances and Mr. Klinger made sure we were well prepared. So by springtime we were all champing at the bit to let everyone hear how well we played.

These concerts were popular events, and the seats were filled for each performance. We were roughly a fifty-piece orchestra, and we knew that few things thrilled Mr. Klinger more than a topnotch performance from us. For however long he'd been the school's musical director, it appeared that he enjoyed these concerts more than anyone. He was one of those very dramatic conductors who provided an exciting visual element to his conducting. Since everything always went according to plan, before we got to the middle of our opening piece, I would see beads of sweat starting to form and glisten on Mr. Klinger's forehead. Seeing this and by watching his own little performance at the conductor's podium, we always knew that we were giving him what he wanted; and that made us play even better. There was a very good give and take between us. We fed from his boundless energy, and he fed from what we gave him back with our instruments. As he waved, gestured, pointed, punched, slashed, and jabbed at the air, he was able to raise and lower the intensity, dynamics, and volume of the music. I sat right in front of him in the woodwind section; so I saw what he was capable of as a conductor from close up as he led us through our fine collection of songs.

At the end of each performance Mr. Klinger's shirt, face, and head would be soaked with sweat. Then, to the thunderous applause and standing ovations, he would signal us to stand and bow to the audience with him. It was all done with quality music and professionalism as our highest priorities.

With so many good things happening for me, I was very concerned about my mother's plan to move. As much as she wanted to move and given my resistance, we both very carefully danced around the touchy subject even though we both knew it was still on the table and needed to be resolved. South Carolina was fun for me when I was much younger, but I knew that it could hardly replace the things I enjoyed in NYC as a teenager.

Though I never asked her why she was so set on uprooting and moving away, I have a strong hunch, now, that it could have had something to do with a problem taking place in our neighborhood. Though yellowish-brown stains on fingertips had long been one of the less visible signs that marijuana had become a popular mood-altering substance for many, when heroin hit the street with a much more noticeable impact, it marked the end of an era in our neighborhood, Harlem, and much of NYC, not to mention the lives, hopes, and dreams of many.

Given the way that heroin had been laying waste to the neighborhood, it was likely that my mother's concern for us was causing her to have second thoughts about life in the big city. Though we never really talked about it, I am sure she saw the sad turn of events taking place in our beautiful neighborhood. Not only that, but she saw just how possible it was for peer pressure to cause some of the best kids to find themselves in trouble by trying to follow the crowd or by trying to grow up too soon.

But for me, with school, music, good summer jobs, an effective junior high school drug prevention class, a good upbringing, good friends, and a good family, curiosity about heroin was not even a passing thought for me, or my siblings. Despite peer pressure's formidable nature, when it came to my health, safety, and well being, I was never much of a risk taker by any means.

At the height of our swimming craze, when my friends took to jumping off the 125th Street Pier to swim in the Hudson River and repeatedly calling for me to join them ("Come on in Burrell, the water is fine"), I wanted no part of it. Then after almost blowing a hole in my chest trying to find the meaning of smoking pleasure, good judgment finally prevailed, and I put an end to smoking before it was too late. When hitching rides on the back of buses while on bicycles, roller skates, or just jumping on and holding onto the tail light with their hands (and their feet on the bumpers) for short rides were the latest daring things to do, I could not help but think of the price that would be paid for the slightest mistake. There was a time when kids took to tying ropes around pieces of steel wool and lighting matches to them. Then they would spin it around above their heads in our front yard at night. This sent sparks flying out in a circle that bounced when they hit the ground. It looked like a water fountain or a lasso made of yellow sparks. It was creative, pretty, and it seemed like a lot of fun, but it was a little bit too risky for me. The idea of one of those sparks landing in my shirt pocket or ear was enough to keep me from joining in on the risky fun. So I watched it all from a safe distance and never tried it firsthand. Even at Coney Island, I could never understand the thrill everyone seemed to get from roller coaster rides and spook houses. I tried them each once, and I never did either one again.

So when the heroin crisis hit and shook our neighborhood to its core, I wanted no part of it. With the ensuing problems of crime, overdose, and the loss of so many hopes and dreams (if these were, in fact, my mother's concerns), I can't blame her at all. But as I said, as far as I could tell, there was nothing about my siblings and me that showed our judgment on things like this was lacking.

One summer our entire neighborhood was shocked when one of our friends died from a heroin overdose at no more than 15 years old. The kid's mother and my mothers were close friends, so this tragic event may have struck a bit too close for comfort for my mother. He was found in his bathtub in a semiconscious state, and despite the efforts made to revive him, his life could not be saved.

During this time my sister, Doris, had just returned to the United States from Germany with her son, Duane. Since her husband had a few months left to his tour of duty, the plan was for her to come back to set things up for their lives here. They lived with us while Doris worked at Harlem's Knickerbocker Hospital.

One evening Doris was attacked while on her way in or out of our building, and the assailant stole her purse. He roughed her up quite a bit, too; but we were never able to determine who did it. It didn't seem that it was anyone from our building, because we knew everyone; and she could have easily pointed the person out to us. So the chances were good that it was an outsider lurking around and looking for a chance to mug someone in our neighborhood, and unfortunately Doris was in the wrong place at the wrong time. With our address in her purse, remarkably, he sent the purse back to us with all of Doris' important papers, but he kept the money. Apparently, this mugger had a small code of ethics that he lived by, was more sadistic than we thought, or had a very odd sense of humor. Be that as it may, all of this could have been a big concern for my mother, and it was a clear indicator of this dismal problem that had settled upon and engulfed our neighborhood. Given how bad and dangerous things had become, our friendly milkman stopped delivering everyone's ice-cold bottles of milk in the morning.

As the heroin crisis tightened its grip, we saw the youthful sparkle in many of our friends' eyes go out and turn into two deep lifeless pits at the front of their heads. Then too, the corners of their mouths started to droop down and turn into what looked like upside down smiles that we called "the beast," It also caused their eyes to bug out in a hideous glare from time to time. "The beast" were not only the words used to describe these upside down smiles and glares, but it was also another way of saying that the heroin was doing what their users wanted it to do for them. Along with this beastly look, heroin caused its users to have incessant bouts of itching and scratching. We regularly saw people scratching their noses, legs, arms, and other body parts in somewhat uninhibited ways. So if we saw someone leaning, nodding, or scratching with the corners of their mouths drooping down, and their eyes bugging out, there was no question about what was happening; and I am sure that none of it got past my mother's watchful eyes.

The quinine that was used to cut the strength of the heroin was said to leave a bitter taste in one's mouth. As a result, this caused people to drink sodas to kill the bad taste. So along with that additional clue, if we saw this array of signs and symptoms, there was an expression we had that described it all. We would say that the person was "beast to the buttered roll." This was a phrase that we started to hear and use, more and more, as the heroin crisis worsened.

One other unmistakable sign of heroin use was the unusual way that it caused people to throw up. As we saw all too often, just as casually as someone would turn their head to the side to cough, many took a second or two to turn to the side to hurl right onto the sidewalk while people walked by with their children. There would be no forewarning, coughing, or gagging when this happened. Instead, like silent geysers, we saw the gastric contents of heroin users erupt and spill out and onto the ground all the time. Then unfazed, the person would casually wipe the area around their mouths with the back of a sleeve and continue with what they were doing as if nothing had happened. So despite the good things our neighborhood and Fun City had to offer, the heroin crisis was something that we could have done without; and it was something that Grant's security guards and police officers were unable to protect many of its young people from.

The magnitude of the problem had grown to such an extent that at the end of the dances, the men's bathroom floors, urinals, and toilets turned into pools of tossed cookies. Given Gregory's way with words and his comedic timing, he described the tragic scene in the men's bathroom to me in a way that only he could. While talking about it one day, he told me that when you go to the bathroom at the dances now, you don't even have to walk to the urinals any more. As he put it, all you had to do was put your heel on the floor just inside the door, push off from the wall, and you would slide across the floor to the other side.

Bearing witness to so much blight, like young self-appointed drug counselors, many of us tried our best to get our fallen friends to come to their senses. But, time and time again, we would always get the same reply: "I'm not going to get hooked on this stuff, it hardly gets me high." But they had no idea of what they were up against. As they continued to dabble, it was not long before their lives would be turned completely upside down, and everything that came with getting their next fix was the only thing they lived for.

At first they would sniff or "snort" the powdery substance with a fingernail file right out of the small plastic bags it was sold in. Many snorted it so much that it burned holes through the membrane that separates each nostril. As their tolerance for that continued to go up, they started to inject it under their skin; this was called "skin popping." Then when skin-popping no longer gave them the ride they wanted, they moved on to shooting it directly into their veins, and this was called "mainlining."

Once someone had reached that point, they were well beyond any words of advice that we had to offer. Though heroin use was something new for the neighborhood, when the needles entered the picture that was the real game changer; there were loads of other tools and accessories ("the works") that came into play at that point. Spoons were needed to cook the heroin in water with a match or a lighter. Then there would be belts or anything else that could be used to tie around an arm to make their veins easier to get to. The corners of the basketball courts, where many of these same kids once passionately played basketball, became very popular places for these heroin use procedures and rituals.

Along with the hellhole heroin caused so many to spiral down into, the grief it caused parents was sad to see. Nonetheless, with much dignity, these parents continued to hold their heads high and worked hard to provide for their families. Many of them were single mothers, and they did what they could to make the best of the horrible situation. I do not know if drug rehabilitation programs existed at that time, but I never heard of anyone being treated by one. The closest thing to a drug rehabilitation program was a jail cell. If someone were arrested for possession, they had no choice but to kick their habit, cold turkey, behind bars. Then when they were released, with every intention of staying clean, as soon as they came back to the people and places where it all started, they would soon find themselves in the same situation over and over again. The jails were like revolving doors for many of our friends. In spite of it all, I used to see these agonized parents going back and forth to work, only to have their children steal money, household items and anything else that would help them get their next fix, or "nickel bag." I didn't understand the magnitude of what these parents must have felt then as much as I do now. Had I a better sense of what they had to endure, I would have tried to make some kind of gesture, or at least offer a word or two of support to these heartbroken, bewildered, and devoted parents. I must add, too, that many of my friends and others had the strength, character, and fortitude to pull themselves out of this tough situation that had been thrown into their paths, and they are now living very good, healthy, happy, and productive lives. Unfortunately though, this was not the case for everyone. Without question, this was Fun City's seedy underbelly.

Despite the devastating effect heroin use had on the neighborhood, or whatever it was that concerned my mother, we finally reached a settlement about this idea of moving. After one or two more attempts to convince me to move, she saw how much it distressed me; and, much to my relief, she shelved the idea of moving, for good.

8

Epiphany, Better Late Than Never

With that life altering hurtle out of the way, and my high school years winding down, I experienced an awakening that resulted in a complete change in my lukewarm attitude about school and academic matters. Until that time, my last day of school could have not come soon enough. I was convinced that graduation would mark the end of school for me forever. My plan was to get a job, play music, and wash my hands of anything having to do with formal education. But my thinking on this changed, and it made studying and learning more important, appealing, and interesting to me than ever before. I am not sure of what brought all of this on, but what had long seemed like an obligatory and burdensome chore ceased to be so. It were as if a part of my brain, that had been in hibernation, had finally decided to wakeup.

It could have been the realization that my twelve years of schooling was coming to an end, and made it no longer the endless daily grind that it once seemed. Or it could have been that I would soon be getting out to face the world as an adult for the first time. Whatever it was, the problem with my newly found appreciation for learning was the fact that it had come a bit late, to say the least. The hard and cold fact of the matter was that I had run out of time, and I knew that it was going to be impossible for me to make up for the time I'd lost. Then to make matters worse, I realized more than ever that I had been pushed through a marginal educational process that left me with much less than I should have had at the end of twelve years, and there was nothing I could do about it. Given my less than exemplary grades, classes, and transcripts, the idea of applying to a college or university was out of the question. So it was a very sad and sobering reality for me to accept the fact that I had wasted so much valuable time and had so little to show for it, other than a symbolic and, pretty much, worthless general high school diploma.

When the full weight of my situation hit me, I was so desperate to do something about it that I took a ferryboat to Staten Island to pick up an application for Staten Island Community College. The long and slow ride gave me time to think. During the ride, I promised myself to work as hard as I could if I were able to get into S.I.C.C. But while looking over the admission requirements on the way back, I realized that I didn't have a snowball's chance of getting in. So before the boat made it halfway back to Manhattan, I'd decided not to fill it out. Then for the rest of the way I thought long and hard about my future and tried to find a way out of this distressful situation I had suddenly found myself in.

Though my education was good and fulfilling in many ways, in the end, the suspicion I had about it was very real and it hit me like a brick. It was indeed like a conveyor belt that brought many of us in and shipped us out practically empty handed. Then if that were not enough for me to think about, there was something else hanging over my head that made my dire situation that much more pressing. This had to do with the military draft and how quickly the army was snatching kids like me up, and shipping us off to Vietnam soon after leaving high school. If a high school graduate were able to get into a college or university and carry a full load of classes, a student deferment would keep him from being drafted. But in most cases, student deferments and college educations were well beyond the reach of young people from low income and working-class families.

During my second year in high school, a teacher talked to us about the Vietnam War. This was the first time I'd ever heard of Vietnam. Not only had I never heard of Vietnam, but I had no idea that a war was going on. As I continued to hear more about Vietnam, I saw how quickly guys older than me were being scooped up and shipped out. I saw, too, how my conveyor belt of an educational system worked in favor of the Selective Service. If a young man were 18 years old, no longer in school, had two arms, two legs, no mental health issues, no drug problems, did not have flat feet or asthma, and was heterosexual, the selective service very much wanted to have a word with him. I sidestepped the heroin crisis, but the military draft was another story; like a charging bull, it was imposing, in my path, and coming right at me.

As the war raged on, and as the pros and cons were argued, we all heard that if anyone refused military service it would be a blemish on their "personal record." With this blemish, it was our understanding that getting a job would be very difficult if not impossible. Then along with that, it was very likely that the person would have to serve jail time for it too.

Along with this educational enlightenment I experienced, I had also developed more of a sense of things going on in the larger world around me. Music was still important to me, but the scope with which I now saw the world and life had broadened. With relatively small pockets of resistance to the war taking shape and the war's continued expansion, I too started to form my own opinions about it; and crawling around in a jungle at 18 years old on the other side of the world did not add up in my book, regardless of the angle I tried to look at it. So with the Selective Service nipping at my heels, schoolwork, studying, and education seemed more attractive to me than ever before.

Roughly six months before graduating, my long-awaited Selective Service notice arrived in the mail; and it felt as if my heart had dropped to the floor when I saw it. Right then I knew that it was all very real, and that I was now a part of the process. This was some kind of welcome to adulthood as far as I was concerned. Never once did I think that something so daunting, bizarre, and unsettling would be waiting for me at the end of my high school years. Twelve years of school to be tossed out and onto a battlefield was more than a rude awakening for me. These Selective Service notices essentially informed us that they knew who we were, and that it was time to go to the induction center to register and to take a physical exam.

On the morning of my physical examination, I thought if I could get my old asthma condition to flare up, the doctor would reject me for medical reasons and place me into the 4-F category. If I knew then what I know now, all I would have had to do was close myself off somewhere for fifteen minutes with dust, cigarette smoke, or a house cat, and my asthma would have kicked in immediately. Instead, I jogged from the front of my building to the train station to work up a sweat in the cold morning air. When I was younger, this would have brought on an asthma attack, without fail. But this time, much to my disappointment, along with becoming sweaty and even colder, there was not even the slightest hint of an asthma attack. In fact, when I reached the train station, my air passages were so clear that my breathing was better than usual. Clear air passages and a healthy heart rate, not withstanding, it was a tough time for me, and it seemed as if things in my life had suddenly taken a turn that was not so good.

The drab and depressing Selective Service building was jam-packed with guys my age; and the dismal room we were in looked and felt like the locked ward of a psychiatric hospital. It was clear that many of the guys there had been thinking of ways to avoid being drafted too. While we waited for our names to be called, I saw guys behaving in all kinds bizarre ways, in an effort to be declared unstable, thus unfit to serve. But it was clear that the Selective Service staff had seen it all before, and they saw right through anything that was contrived. So if someone's plan was not airtight or if they came anywhere close to what the Selective Service wanted, they could expect to get what we all dreaded: a 1-A draft classification notice.

After my physical exam, I left the building feeling dejected and even depressed. I was sure that I had passed my physical exam. I struggled with exams throughout my years in school and had my health issues as a child, but when it came to my physical exam with the Selective Service, I was a brilliant and glowing picture of health. Now the only thing left for me to do was to wait to receive my official draft classification notice by mail. Within a week, my classification notice arrived; and, just as I had expected, I passed and was classified as 1-A. In other words, I was fit and eligible for military service. My last ray of hope was the military's lottery system; if my lottery number were high enough, I would not be drafted. I don't remember exactly how the numbers ran, but (as an example) if someone's number were three hundred or above, the chances were good that they would not be drafted. On the other hand, if someone's number were anything below that, they were as good as gone. So if three hundred were the cutoff point, my number was roughly two hundred-fifty.

As I continued to try to find a solution of some kind, I looked into a program called Young Life; Young Life was part of an organization called the Neighborhood Youth Corp. They provided various kinds of support services for young adults in my neighborhood and other parts of Harlem. My sister had been involved in Young Life's other activities, and this was how I learned about it. Based in the community active Church of the Master, it consisted of several components. Of the two programs I remember, one took young adults camping and on trips to places as far away as Colorado, and the other one dealt with educational matters. This component provided academic assistance by way of a program called the Harlem Street Academy.

So if someone like me came up short, scholastically, at the end of the road and wanted to do something about it, Harlem's Young Life Street Academy was right there to provide us with the classes and tutoring we needed. So during the summer months, after I graduated, I enrolled into the Harlem Street Academy program and worked hard to catch up on math, English, biology, social studies, and anything else that I did not get in much of a quality way during my high school years. Even though the Harlem Street Academy could not keep me out of the clutches of the Selective Service, I enjoyed being in a learning environment and studying again. After seeing me struggle for so long, it made my mother happy to see this change in me.

The director of the Harlem Street Academy was a wonderful woman we called Dr. Bryant. She was an African-American woman, and she was like a second mother to all of us. She looked after each and every one of us with a remarkable amount of care and attention. In spite of there being so many of us, she knew us all by name, and she always found time to be sure we were getting everything we needed from the program. There was a Jamaican man who tutored us who we called "Mr. G." He was the only tutor we had, but he was very smart and he could tutor large groups of us in any subject we needed help with. Then too, with ease, he was able to teach and tutor several subjects at the same time.

During my time at the Harlem Street Academy, Dr. Bryant seemed to notice how hard I'd been working and how serious I was about my work. As a result, I was one of the students chosen to enroll into a private college preparatory school in Newark, New Jersey called Newark Prep. So finding out about and having access to the Harlem Street Academy and Newark Prep were two strokes of luck for me, when I needed them more than anything. It was more than anything I could have ever asked for. Additionally, being a student at Newark Prep would keep me from being drafted as long as I carried a full load of classes and maintained good grades.

This was perfect for me in so many ways; we even received a weekly stipend, and our books and tuition were paid for too. I would have gladly done it without the stipend, but the extra money made it even better. The only thing Dr. Bryant asked of us was that we work hard and that we be at the bus on time every morning for the one hour ride across the George Washington Bridge to Newark, New Jersey. Given all that we got in return, it was very little to ask of us, as far as I was concerned. So like clockwork, Monday through Friday, in rain, sunshine, heat, hail, sleet, or snow, we were all at the bus bright and early, and ready to go.

For the next two years, my sister and I, along with a cast of characters from our neighborhood and all over Harlem, were involved in the educational experience of a lifetime. Newark Prep was an excellent school, and for being the private and prestigious school that it is, I always felt very comfortable and welcomed there. We arrived in a bright yellow school bus every day, but not once did I have the impression that we were thought of or treated as a collection of disadvantaged misfits and outcasts from Harlem. The director of the school was a man named Mr. Garson. He was a very fair, but a no nonsense guy when it came to his school. Then when it came to his teaching staff, it was clear that he hired the very best teachers he could find. Academically, my two years at Newark Prep surpassed my six years of junior high and high school threefold.

To say the least, the teachers were the absolute best. Not only were they enthusiastic about teaching and knowledgeable, but they were able to engage us in a remarkable way. Two worlds came together nicely. The teachers were, likely, middle to upper middle class, and probably from the affluent suburbs of New Jersey. We, on the other hand, were a varied assortment of inner city African-American kids from Harlem, complete with all of the rough edges of inner-city life. Despite our very different backgrounds, we pursued a path of teaching and learning that was more than noteworthy.

Our English teacher's name was Mrs. Brogan. With her silver hair rolled into a bun at the back of her head, she reminded me of the profile of the woman on the Camay soap bar. Impeccably dressed, she was a true picture of elegance, class, and style. My first impression of her was that of a strict piano teacher who would harshly crack a ruler over a student's knuckles for poor playing technique, or someone who would quickly cross to the other side of the street to avoid walking too closely to one of us, but those impressions faded quickly with her first few words. While, very easily, being one of the kindest, most sophisticated, and gracious individuals that I have ever met, she seemed to have the heart of a lioness too. She was not afraid of, uncomfortable around, or intimidated by any of us (or anyone else for that matter). She was always poised, calm, and collected. So in her classroom there was no mistake about who was in charge, and we all knew it; not once did she ever have to step out of character to admonish any of us for anything. We all knew we were in her classroom to learn. Even the most attention seeking, clownish, or thuggish individuals in our group knew that her classroom was hardly the place for their antics. So without her ever having to cast as much as one sideways glance, we all knew what was expected of us when she closed the door to get her English classes underway.

Mrs. Brogan made no bones about her love for English and grammar. It was clear that the rules and nuances of grammar fascinated her to no end. I had never heard anyone speak so fondly and glowingly of English before. Until that time, the only thing I'd ever heard anyone say about English was how much they disliked it or that it was their worse subject; it was like a mantra that people seemed to chant by rote. But Mrs. Brogan spoke about English in the way that people speak about their love for food, literature, art, music, theatre, poetry, and sports. She lived for good grammar, good vocabulary, and good word usage; and her enthusiasm was catching. I never knew studying English could be so much fun.

We explored grammar in great detail. This was something that none of my previous English teachers had ever done. Before going to Newark Prep, I had never diagramed a sentence. But in Mrs. Brogan's class we broke sentences down, isolated and analyzed their various parts of speech, and learned the rules about subject/verb agreement. I learned about prepositions, prepositional phrases, adjectives, nouns, pronouns, infinitives, parenthetical expressions, articles, reflexive verbs, punctuation, adverbs, the subjunctive mood, and the purposes they all serve and the correct way to use them. There were two very good books we used. One was The Elements of Style, and the other one was The Plain English Handbook. They were like Mrs. Brogan's Bibles, and I still have my copy of The Plain English Handbook; and recently, I bought a copy of The Elements of Style.

We studied these books from cover to cover without skipping one page; and unlike before, my focus was razor sharp and very much on point; I did no daydreaming while in class, and I was never on the wrong pages of the books we worked from. Then before long, I found myself just as enchanted and fascinated by English as Mrs. Brogan. I started to pay more attention to how I spoke, and I tried to keep all of the useful things in mind that I'd been learning in her class. Then too, along with my ongoing effort to add new Spanish words to my collection, inspired and impressed by Mrs. Brogan's eloquence, it became clear to me that my English vocabulary could use some fine tuning, too. It was a pleasure having her as my teacher, and I looked forward to being in her classroom every day. Her impact on me was profound; and as I later realized, these valuable nuts and bolts of English grammar made learning Spanish a lot easier for me.

We had another very good teacher who taught Spanish and French, and his name was Mr. Camiscolli (or Mr. C. as he told us he liked to be called on our first day in his class). At Newark Prep we were able to choose the language that we wanted to study. In the exact opposite way Mrs. Brogan made her classroom a perfect place for learning (with her polite, respectful, and no-nonsense approach), Mr. C. did the same thing with the relaxed and informal setting he provided us with.

With learning Spanish being as important as it has been to me, I liked Mr. C. right away. He did not appear to be much older than us, but as young as he was, he was impressive as a person and a skillful teacher. He spoke Spanish very well, and he made learning it an enjoyable process. If one of us did not understand something, he would be sure that we all had it before he moved on. As a result, no one ever felt uncomfortable about asking him to stop to explain something again. So, in great detail, we explored Spanish grammar, vocabulary, accent, tense, verb conjugation, reading, and writing. He and Mrs. Brogan were like Mr. Kamermeyer all over again. It was clear that he enjoyed having us as his students, and he clearly understood the disadvantages and challenges we faced. Then too, and perhaps most importantly, we could tell that he supported us in every way, and we could tell that he wanted the very best for all of us during our two years with him as our Spanish teacher.

There were other excellent teachers like Mr. Murray, the history teacher, and several others whose names I have forgotten. But they, too, very skillfully guided us through the rigors of algebra, geometry, biology, and social studies, subjects that stimulate, stretch, strengthen, and massage our brains in ways that everyone should experience.

Studying algebra, and geometry at Newark Prep was enjoyable for me too. In high school, I was curious about these more advanced forms of math, but I was never allowed to take any of them. But by the time I was a student at Newark Prep, my curiosity had quadrupled, and I was more than ready to give them a shot. So like a fish to water, I plunged into them with everything I had, and I soaked things up like a sponge. During my two years at Newark Prep, I did not miss one day of school. I did very well with my classes, and I had more fun than ever studying, learning, and taking tests. The teachers at Newark Prep unlocked and stimulated parts of my brain and thinking that had been touched only once and very briefly in the sixth grade with Mr. Kamermeyer.

I do not remember how, but for two of my summer vacations, I landed a pretty sweet job working for Pan American Airlines. The large Met Life Building in the middle of Park Avenue (right above Grand Central Station, on 42nd St.) was the Pan Am Building at that time. Our band was doing very well, and we played just about every weekend. So, in total, I had a good summer job, I played music on the weekends, and I was in school. More important to me than that was the fact that the Selective Service was off my back for the time being. I was 18 years old, and because 36 years of age was the cutoff point for being drafted, I was still not out of the woods by any means. Nonetheless, I was committed to studying hard while enjoying the way things had been going for me, and I made it a point not to worry about the Selective Service until the time came.

Without a doubt, I was more than willing to do whatever was needed or asked of me at my job. But what I needed to do had to be done soon after I arrived and at the end of the day. My work had to do with computers back when they were the size of refrigerators. I had no idea of what they were used for, nor did I have a full picture of the purpose that my job served half the time. But, I never made any mistakes, and I heard the word "delete" for the first time while I was being trained. With so little for me to do, I used to sit at my desk drinking coffee, eating bagels, reading the New York Times, and talking with my interesting co-workers from around the world and from all over NYC, including a woman from Argentina named Elsa Palacios (who I enjoyed practicing speaking Spanish with) who I took a special liking to, in spite of the fact that she was quite a few years older than me.

When the boredom of doing practically nothing all day became unbearable, I started to take the elevator downstairs to look at the books and magazines in Grand Central Station's magazine shops, or walk around inside Grand Central Station. When I became bored with that, I started to go outside of the air-conditioned building to explore Midtown in the sweltering heat wrapped in my suits, shirts, and neckties. I would spend the day people watching and mingling with the New York City worker bees that made the city run. When I became tired of that, I'd call either Frankie or Angelo (our singer and trombone player) to get together with one of them for lunch. Angelo worked a few blocks from me, and Frankie worked on Wall Street. When Angelo and I got together, I used to ride with him in his car as he made his inter-office mail deliveries. Then we would have lunch, hang out in Central Park or in other parts of Midtown. Other times I would go with him to visit his parents in Spanish Harlem while we talked and joked about anything worth a good laugh.

Being the prankster that Angelo is, when we were in Spanish Harlem one of his favorite gags started with him spotting some unsuspecting person. Then, if we were on a small street with no cars behind us, he would slow his car down, open the door, and drag his foot on the ground while he pushed the break pedal with his other foot. To the people watching from the sidewalk, it appeared as if he were stopping the car by dragging his foot on the ground. He would then (in Spanish) ask someone for directions to the nearest service station. Then he would tell them that his breaks were not working and that he has to stop the car by dragging his foot on the ground. He would say it so convincingly that his gag worked every time as people watched in horror, hearing his tall tale.

Angelo liked to put me on the spot too whenever he caught me off guard. If there were people walking in front of us and a place for him to hide, he would let loose with a loud and startling scream, and would quickly disappear by hiding in the place that he had previously staked out. Then when the startled people turned around to see what nut was carrying on so outrageously, I would be the only one left standing there.

So whatever Angelo and I spent the day doing while roaming the streets of Manhattan, by four o'clock I would be back at my desk to set up the computer index cards to close out the books for the day. It did not bother my boss or any of my co-workers that I was out of the office for such long periods of time, so by midsummer of my first year, that was how I spent my working hours during those two summer vacations. Angelo was pretty amazed by this, and would always say to me, "My God, what kind of job is it that you have where you can stay outside like that all day, and still get paid for it?"

If we had a gig on a night before we had to be at work early the next day, we would get home at 3 or 4 o'clock in the morning, sleep for what seemed like ten minutes, get up, and drag ourselves to work. Then when we got together or talked on the phone, Angelo would always tell me that he was so tired and sleepy that it felt as if he had clothespins on his eyes.

This was my very good friend and funny band mate, Angelo Rodriguez. I would enjoy sitting down with him now for a good talk and plenty of laughs about all the fun we had playing music back during our Orchestra Flamboyan days. He was a real character, a great guy, a lot of fun, and perfect to have as a member of our band.

9

Orq. Flamboyan
for Your Dancing Pleasure

As a band, our hard work and dedication continued to bring us good things. As more people heard us, calls for playing engagements came in all the time. We played gigs all over the city and one as far away as a fancy resort in Upstate New York called Villa Sol. Given the high visibility that came with playing Latin music in NYC during that time, whenever Frankie thought he saw someone looking at him for more than four or five seconds, he would gleefully rub his hands together and tell me that someone had just recognized him; and, to that, I would always say, " Sure Frankie." He seemed to enjoy that aspect of playing music as much as he enjoyed singing, and he shamelessly and humorously did nothing to hide his feelings about it. He absolutely loved the attention, and if someone asked him if he was the singer for Orchestra Flamboyan, it would take him the rest of the day to stop talking about it. Like Angelo, Gregory, Ellsworth, Chickie, Milton, and Kenny, Frankie was another character, and I had a lot of fun with him sampling his mother's excellent cooking while talking about music, before going out to the various clubs to connect with promoters and club owners on the weekends that we were not playing.

We played almost every weekend and often on Sunday or Thursday nights when we had to be up early for work or school the next morning. Fueled by youth, enthusiasm, and our love for music, very often we'd get home at daybreak after playing a string of gigs that ended at one of the after-hours clubs in Spanish Harlem. More often than not, we would play a set or two at one venue, pack up our instruments, get our pay, and then dash off to another club to play our second and (often) third gig for the night. This was just how active the Latin music scene was in NYC during that time; and bands with much higher name recognition than ours played even more. After this marathon, we would return home exhausted and exhilarated. I don't know how we did it, but we loved every moment of it. The more gigs we had, the later we got home, and the later we got home the more tired we were. Then the more tired we were, the more we loved it; and with the crew of characters we were fortunate enough to have in the band, it was a seemingly endless cycle of music, fun, adventure, laughs, and good times.

A major milestone for us came when we played on a bill with a popular singer named Joe Quijano and his band. Joe Quijano's albums were a part of my LP record collection, so sharing the stage with a talent of that stature was more than exciting for us. But a couple of things caught us (and me in particular) unexpectedly on the night of this groundbreaking engagement.

Near the end of the night, a fight broke out in the middle of the dance floor. Never experiencing anything like this before, we were not sure of what to do. So we continued playing, hoping that things would soon calm down; but things went from bad to worse. When I noticed that something was wrong, I was at the microphone and in the middle of one of my flute solos. I saw a guy holding another guy by the back of his head and neck. He had the guy hoisted up on his back in an odd way, and was trying to flip him over and down onto the floor. The guy being tossed was upside-down with his feet dangling in mid-air as he teetered back and forth for what seemed like a full ten seconds. Eventually he lost the tug-of-war, and came crashing down, hard, to the floor. Then the entire place broke out into a full-scale brawl, with fists, bottles, chairs, and drinks flying everywhere while we continued playing. So instead of playing for a jam-packed ballroom filled with festive dancers, we were playing for a crowd who were throwing roundhouses and haymakers at each other like there was no tomorrow. With the fight far from over and getting worse by the minute, for our safety, we decided to stop playing to get away from the middle of the stage.

By the time the police arrived and restored order, all of our instruments were packed. Then amid the overturned tables, chairs, and spilled drinks, we stood on the dance floor waiting to be paid. While standing next to a table of food that, miraculously, was still upright, I take no pride in saying that I scooped up a handful of pork-fried rinds, shoved them into my mouth, and started to chew. The pork-fried rinds were so dry and salty that they made me thirsty. I looked around for a soda, but there were no sodas left. The only thing I found was a cooler with cans of beer in a pool of water from melted ice. Celebrating our groundbreaking gig with a few more drinks than usual, I had no intention of touching any more alcohol for the rest of the night. But because I was so thirsty, I gave into my thirst, plunged my hand into the water, and pulled out a can of beer. Then I popped the cap, took two swallows, and threw the can and the rest of the beer into a garbage can nearby.

After we were paid, Gregory, Kenny, Ellsworth, and I said goodbye to the others and headed to the train station with the two girls who came to hear us play. While walking, I realized that the two chugs of beer may have been just enough to push me over the edge, but I thought and hoped that I would be fine. After getting myself seated on the train, it was not long before I realized that drinking the beer was a big mistake and that my worse fear might just come to pass. As it turned out, it would have been better for me to drink the water from the melted ice in the cooler. As the train chugged along shaking from side to side with the beer, alcohol, and pork-fried rinds sloshing around in my stomach, I knew that I would be lucky if I made it to 125th Street before my stomach turned inside out.

When I realized I was not going to make it, to avoid embarrassing myself, sickening my band mates, sickening the other people on the train, and sickening the two girls (one of whom I liked and hoped to impress with our groundbreaking gig), I quickly got up from my seat with my flute case tucked tightly under my arm and stumbled to the door leading to the space between the two train cars. I pulled the door open and stepped into the small area just in time. Then I carefully closed the door behind me and wasted no time spray-painting that area and the tracks below with a cone-shaped spew of beer, alcohol, and partially digested pork-fried rinds. Given the horrible shape I was in, I was lucky that I didn't drop my flute case down onto the train tracks. Mortified beyond words but feeling slightly better, I stumbled back to my seat against the movement of the loud, clattering, and fast moving train. At that point, the only thing I could think of was getting to my bed. But with several stops to go, I knew that it was going to be a while before I would be able to embrace the comfort of my soothing bed and pillow. Given the horrible condition I was in, I couldn't even walk the two girls home. Then the one final obstacle I faced was getting by my mother who either slept lightly or stayed up until she knew that I had arrived home safely.

Before opening the door, I did my best to steady myself to conceal the horrible shape I was in. I opened the door quietly, stepped inside, and saw that all of the lights were out. With my ears working like radar, I did my best to determine if my mother was awake. Then, much to my relief and good fortune, all was quiet on the home front, and my mother was fast asleep. I tiptoed past her room, slipped out of my clothes, and landed on my bed just as my bed and bedroom started to spin in opposite directions. Fortunately for me, I was out cold before the spinning became unbearable. I had long heard people talk about hangovers, and I had finally gotten a chance to see just how bad they are the next morning. It was a tough but very good lesson, and it easily convinced me to never let it happen again. And although it was the alcohol that made me sick, it was the very last time that I had ever, as much as, placed a finger on a pork-fried rind. In the grand scheme of things, the night was a feather in our cap as a band, but the fight, the two swigs of beer, and its consequences were things I could have done without.

There was another time when we had the honor of sharing the stage with one of the best bands to come out of the Latin music scene of the early 60s in NYC. This was when we shared the stage with Eddie Palmieri and his band, Conjunto La Perfecta, one true powerhouse of a band if there ever was one. As it turned out, we were not on the bill to play with them, but an idea occurred to me that I thought was just too good to pass on. Eddie Palmieri was going to play at a club called the Palm Garden Ballroom in Midtown, and on that same night, we played on the other side of town. When we finished our gig, we felt very good about how well we played. Given our excitement, I suggested that we go to the Palm Garden Ballroom to talk to the promoters about allowing us to play a tune or two as an audition while Eddie Palmieri and his band took their break.

Clearly, this was not unlike the enthusiasm of an amateur boxer getting the best of him, and causing him to want to jump into the boxing ring with Muhammad Ali during Ali's prime. Despite being the overly ambitious task that it was, we were a pretty bold, enthusiastic, and adventurous bunch. Then too, given how well we played earlier, the other band members liked the idea too. We had a good band for being the ragtag bunch of knuckle-heads we were, and we wanted as many people to hear us as possible, including Eddie Palmieri and his band. Of course we couldn't hold a candle to them. After all, they were not called Conjunto La Perfecta for nothing; they were perfect in every way. Strategically, though, we knew if the promoters liked us, it would give us access to another group of promoters, dancers, and a popular music and dance venue.

After arriving, I went to the two promoters' office. I told them my name and the name of our band. I continued by telling them that we had just played on the other side of town earlier, and I asked them if they would allow us to come in to play a tune or two during Eddie Palmieri's break, as an audition. I mentioned, too, that if they liked us and if they needed a band in the future, they would know we were available to play. A little surprised by my bold request, the two talked it over and decided to let us come in to play.

I left the office, and told everyone that we had been given the green light. As usual the dance floor was jam packed with dancers, so we came through the side entrance to the stage lugging our instruments as we listened to Eddie Palmieri and his band shake the rafters and foundation of the Palm Garden Ballroom with the force of their overwhelming sound. When they finished their set, we greeted Eddie Palmieri and his band members who were great mentors of ours. We worshiped the ground they walked on, and, as usual, they were all there: Ismael Quintana, Tommy Lopez, Barry Rogers, Jorge Castro, Manny Oquendo, Dave Perez, Jose Rodriguez and of course Eddie Palmieri, one of the very best ensembles put together in the history of Latin music (or any other kind of music, for that matter); and they left their mark and legacy wherever they played.

Now we had the unenviable task of taking the stage behind them after another one of their always highly charged and blistering sets of music. In spite of this formidable task that we had taken on for ourselves, not one of our band members had the slightest doubt, hesitance, or nervousness about what we were about to do. We were so lit with enthusiasm about our musical project that we were all quite eager to take the stage at the Palm Garden Ballroom with Eddie Palmieri and his band watching us. I now find it pretty astounding whenever I think of how brash and bold we were to do something like that. With Eddie Palmieri's considerable musical accomplishments and the commanding respect that he has earned for it, barging in on one of his gigs is unheard of; and the chances are good that we were the only band to ever do something so outrageous. Nonetheless, I am ever so grateful that Eddie didn't ask that we be escorted to the club's nearest exit door when the promoters told him why we were there. After the promoters told Eddie what was happening we took the stage, set up, and played two or three songs. Because we had just played two hours earlier and were still warmed up, I am happy to say that we met our challenge quite well. Since Eddie Palmieri's band members watched us from the back of the stage, had we bombed, it would have not been good at all. Not only that, but the Palm Garden crowd was hardly shy; and they took their music and dancing very seriously. So had they not liked us, we would have known about it for sure. But the response from the crowd was good, and they appeared to enjoy dancing to our music. Then just as important to me, it seemed that Eddie Palmieri's musicians liked us too. I made it a point to try to catch any kind of candid reaction from them whenever I could without being too obvious about it; and they seemed to be pleasantly surprised by our performance. Seeing interest, rather than frowns of distaste on their faces was good enough for me. After we finished and before they took the stage again we were able to talk with the musicians of La Perfecta who were all very friendly and supportive. Despite the fact that they were in an altogether different class and category, in no way did I get the impression that they were bothered by the way we barged in on their gig. I even had the chance to spend some time talking with Jorge Castro. I'd spoken with him before plenty of times, but this was the first time he saw me play. He, too, was supportive, and he showed me the tricky fingering positions for two or three very high notes that I didn't know. Though he played the five-key Cuban flute, he knew the modern Boehm flute system too. During my conversation with Jorge Castro, I looked over and saw Gregory talking to Tommy Lopez (Eddie Palmieri's conga player), so this was a special and memorable night of music for us.

While still basking in the glow of our fine performance and my wild idea, when Eddie Palmieri and his band took the stage again, without the slightest hint of competitiveness, vengeance, or a sense of a need to put us in our place, they very respectfully, effortlessly, systematically, and methodically handed our hats to us with their highly polished sound. Gregory and I had a good laugh about it on the way home being the big Eddie Palmieri fans we have always been. In spite of it all, we were still very proud of what we did that night. We knew that we had nothing to be ashamed of since we had played with the very best and had done very well. As you can imagine, our ride home was joyous and filled with much talk about our interesting and eventful night of music. Then most of all, we talked about how our little gambit might pay off for us in the grand scheme of things. The promoters must have liked us, because it resulted in plenty of work for us at the Palm Garden Ballroom. There we played with other popular bands of that time, and other up and coming bands, too, like Mongo Santamaria Jr. and the Lebron Brothers. Then, at some point, the management of the club changed, and the Palm Garden Ballroom became an even more popular NYC club for dancing called The Cheetah.

Another time, I was surprised to see Ray Barretto walk in on one of our gigs at an after-hours club in Spanish Harlem. He too, as I mentioned, had another exciting band called La Moderna. It was about 3 in the morning, and while playing, I watched him from the stage as he walked in to take a seat at the side of the stage to watch and listen to us play. When our set ended, he came over to me and told me how much he liked our band. Then he told me that he was going to play at the Round Table Club that following afternoon, and he invited me to come by; then he asked me to bring my flute. I was thrilled, and told him that I would be there indeed. At the time he had changed his band, and his flute player, Joe Canura, no longer played with him. So, all kinds of thoughts danced in my head about the interesting possibilities that could come from playing with Ray Barretto and his band, even if it were for nothing more than me being able to tell my friends about it.

Gregory went with me the next day, and we entered the high-end Round Table Club on the swanky eastside of Midtown Manhattan. Gregory and I found an empty table and booth, and took seats. Ray and his band were already playing, and as soon as he saw me, he motioned for me to come up to the stage to join them in the song they were playing. I didn't expect him to call me up so suddenly and right in front of everyone. This seemed to shine a spotlight on me in a way that I did not expect or particularly want. Preferably, I would have liked to get myself settled first, and talk to Ray about the song I would be playing in. I knew how bad it would be if they were playing in some obscure or complicated key that I was not comfortable with. The standard keys that I knew, inside and out, were fine for me, but I had no idea what key they were playing in. So, though small, I knew there was potential for an embarrassing problem. It was a roll of the dice that could have gone in one of three ways: very good, so-so, or terribly.

When I saw him waving for me to come up to play and all the attention that it started to attract, I was stricken with a case of cold feet, and I started to have second thoughts about going up to play. So I waved my hand, indicating that I was going to pass on his offer. Despite waving him off, he insisted by gesturing even more animatedly for me to come up to play. By the way he gestured, I could see that he very much wanted me to play. Then Gregory chimed in by telling me to go up to play, too. So the pressure was on at that point, and I had to make a decision quickly, as the people in the club continued to look in my direction, trying to figure out what was happening with Ray and me. I came close to going; but when I thought about it again, I decided not to take the risk. Ray waved again, just as animatedly, calling for me to come up, but in the end I waved him off a final time indicating that I was going to pass. He was disappointed that I bailed out, but I had mixed feelings about it. I was embarrassed that my nerves had gotten the best of me, but I was glad that good judgment on my part won out. With Ray and his band sounding as good as they did, it felt to me as if I caused a major buzz kill to the energy that they had going. But I couldn't help but think of how bad it would have been for me to have this chance to play with Ray Barretto and not play as well as I would have liked. Struggling with a difficult key (playing on the spur of the moment like that) has happened to me before, and there is nothing fun about it at all; and since playing so-so or playing terribly were neither of the alternatives I was interested in, I think I made the right choice. If I'd had a chance to talk with Ray about the song beforehand, I would have played. So I indeed missed out on an opportunity to play with one of the greats. Being the spoiler that I was for Ray and his band, I couldn't bring myself to ask him about playing during his next set. In light of his cordial and personal invitation to me, I did not enjoy distinguishing myself as Ray's buzz kill for the afternoon, but I did sleep well that night, knowing that I did not go running up to the stage to jump into something that I might have not been able to handle. That would have been worse, and it would have haunted me for a long time.

There were two other times when our efforts fell short of the high standards we held ourselves to. On one of these occasions, we played on a boat ride with another popular bandleader, Willie Colon and his band. By all indicators, it seemed to have the makings for a great day of music. Not only were we on the bill with Willie Colon, but it was going to be our first boat ride gig after wanting to play one for some time. Willie Colon was one of our contemporaries, and we (with our bold and overconfident selves) wanted to try to make a name for ourselves by giving him, his band, and his singer, Hector Lavoe, a good run for their money. So as you can see, not only were we bold, but we were competitive, confidant, and even a little bit outrageous with it too. The weather at the South Ferry that day could have not been better. The sun was bright, and the dancers were lined up at the boat's ramp and more than ready to get the festivities underway; and we were, too.

Because the boat's piano was always near water, in horrible shape, and clearly never taken care of, it was flat and way out of tune. There were even a few crucial keys that did not work at all, and some keys were missing altogether right in the middle of the keyboard. When I sat at the piano to tune my flute, I saw the horrible condition that the battered and weather-beaten instrument was in. Then when I tried to tune my flute to it, I could not get the notes to match at all. So I knew, right then that we had a big problem; and worst than that, I had no idea how to solve it.

When we started to play, instead of hearing what I usually hear, I heard something else that sounded like a train wreck with musical instruments. It sounded as if the band had gone in one direction and the piano had wandered off in another direction on its own. As good a piano player as Ellsworth is, it was impossible for him to do anything with it. In all my life, I had never heard anything that sounded so strange. It was a dissonant cacophony that was an assault on the human ear. Then given this odd, embarrassing, and horrible situation we found ourselves in, there was nothing we could do. In hindsight we could have stopped and explained that the piano was hopelessly out of tune, or we could have tried to play without the piano to see how that would have worked. But instead, we did our best to put the best face forward and push through to the end of our long and brutal set. The gig, in the end, was a disaster for us. Perhaps having more experience with this, when Willie Colon and his band took the stage, we saw that his piano player had his own keyboard. So we wrote it off as a tough lesson learned, but learned just a little bit late. Then much later, as happy as I was to learn that Mark Anthony and Jennifer Lopez used the flyer for that boat ride in their movie, that gig did not catch us at our best. As a result, and very soon after, Ellsworth bought a portable electric piano of his own so that this would never happen again.

There was another time when we had to endure the embarrassment of another disastrous performance. But this time, it was particularly bad since we were sharing the stage with, none other than Johnny Pacheco and his band. We had a previous engagement earlier that day in the Coney Island section of Brooklyn, and we were going to be the opening band for Johnny Pacheco later that afternoon at a club called The Corso. Very excitedly we came roaring back to Manhattan to play at this relatively new and very popular club. Our first gig went off without a hitch. We played very well, and I looked forward to playing this second gig for the day. With Johnny Pacheco on the bill, I knew that this would give him a chance to hear us play for the first time. He was one of the founding partners of the Fania Record Company. It was a popular record label at that time, and they were at their peak in popularity. They were signing and recording young and upcoming bands led by Willie Colon, Joe Bataan, and many others. So we very much wanted to leave a good impression with him that day. We were warmed up and more than ready to take the stage. Pre-performance jitters were not an issue for us at all since we'd played so well at our first gig in Brooklyn, and the piano was in mint condition. So what could have possibly gone wrong this time, you might wonder?

When we arrived and started to count heads, I realized that our flaky bass player was nowhere to be found. Somewhat concerned, as unreliable as he'd proven himself to be sometimes, I didn't think for a second that he would stand us up at such an important time, especially since we had played so well earlier, but he did. So with Johnny Pacheco and my, now, new friend Pete "El Conde" Rodriguez present, we were about to take the stage without a bass player. We waited for as long as we could, hoping that he was running late, but he never showed up; and at that point, it was too late to call Buff, our backup bass player.

So now with our start time upon us, and our bass player a no-show, I told Pacheco's bass player about our tough situation. Then I told him that I would pay him if he covered for us on bass for our one set of music. He agreed to do it, and we took the stage with the one glimmer of hope being that we might sound even better with such a good and experienced bass player playing with us. Unfortunately, it did not turn out that way. Given my inexperience writing bass music at that time, he struggled getting through the songs. I didn't know that bass music was written with jazz chord symbols in Latin music. So I used to write it out note for note. Reading bass music that way is a lot harder than reading chord symbols. Chord symbols are like shorthand for bass and piano players; they provide all the information that is needed at one quick glance. So as it happened with our disastrous boat ride gig, when we started to play, the band took off in one direction, and, this time, the bass took off in another direction. In the end, the result was a bad performance. Being the solid troopers we were, we stuck it out to the bitter end. Then embarrassed and disappointed, we left the stage when our set was over. I paid Pacheco's bass player, thanked him for covering, and was happy to start the process of putting the terrible episode behind me.

10

The Cuban Flute
Is Still
Crackin' & Poppin'

When I started to listen to Latin music, the flute played a very important role. Just about as much as the singers, in many cases, the flute was Latin music's much-valued centerpiece. Just about every band had a flute player, and they managed to work the flute into many, if not all of their songs. Tito Puente with his big band style (well known for their outstanding, 6 to 7 piece horn section) reached a wider audience when they changed their musical direction slightly with their most popular song, Oye Como Va. The song is loaded with plenty of good flute playing. This is part and parcel to the considerable influence that charanga had on popular Cuban based and Puerto Rican styled dance music during that time in NYC. Charanga was built around the flute, and I have always seen the flute as the paintbrush that is used to add the special touches and colorings to the canvas created by the other instruments. With the other instruments having the responsibility of locking in with each other and holding the music in place, the flute has the freedom to venture out widely, while soaring high above the music with fewer limitations on what it is allowed to do, given its primary role as an instrument for solos.

In charanga, the singers very often played a secondary role by supporting the flute players with intermittent choruses.

But at some point, the flute started to lose its preeminence as musical trends shifted right under our dancing feet. In place of the hard-hitting Afro-Cuban pulse, that drew me to the music so quickly, a blend of Latin and African-American music started to emerge. Songs were starting to be sung in English, and a dance craze called the Boogaloo found a popular place for itself on New York City's Latin music scene. The Boogaloo, the Wobble, and the Shing-a-ling created a profitable commercial hook for bands, clubs, and record companies; so bands quickly took up this new trend.

In many ways, I liked the idea of these two styles of music coming together. For the first time, I was able to understand all of the words to the songs. Not only that, but it symbolized a cultural blend that I liked that gave birth to a whole new style of music and dance. On the other hand, I was like a jazz purist when it came to Latin music. So, for me, these changes took quite a bit away from this music that I love so much, not to mention the fun and education that came for me, hearing and learning new Spanish words and phrases. So in many respects, I was not all that thrilled with the new direction things had moved in. Then, most of all, this shifting trend started to render the flute more and more obsolete, and it precipitated a steep decline in the popularity of charanga too.

Though the change worked very well for the Joe Cuba Sextet, Johnny Colon, Pete (Boogaloo) Rodriguez, Ricardo Ray, and quite a few other bands, it did not bode well for the more traditional charanga-styled bands. This change started during the mid 60s, and at that time Johnny Pacheco switched from playing the flute to playing percussion and he changed his charanga band to a style called conjunto. In the conjunto style, he used two trumpets instead of violins and flute. I liked that he was one of the few who did not take up the Boogaloo trend, and I liked his new band and his new style of music. But I longed for his charanga band (with its violins and flute that I had, essentially, cut my Latin music teeth on). Whenever I went to see him and his new band, I always asked him to play flute in a song or two, and he always did. Ray Barretto changed his charanga format too by replacing his violin and flute combination with a brass section consisting of one trumpet and one trombone. Charlie Palmieri dropped his violin and flute combination, and replaced it with a brass section too. Mongo Santamaria shifted from playing charanga to playing Latin-jazz, and started to use saxophones and trumpets. Even Eddie Palmieri, well known for his raging trombones and flute combination started to use the flute less. Jorge Castro started to switch between playing flute and trumpet, and eventually the flute and Jorge Castro parted ways with Eddie Palmieri and La Perfecta. Then with one of the patron saints of the five-key flute, Jose Fajardo, living in Florida and Puerto Rico, I was not able to see as many flute players as before.

This shift and the agonizing disappearance of the five-key flute from the NYC Latin music scene weighed on me heavily. It was a tough time for me; and I started to wonder if I had chosen the right instrument. But just before I had lost all hope, in a sudden and unexpected twist of fate, I heard Symphony Sid announce, on his radio program, that Orquesta Broadway was going to play at the Palladium that following weekend. As I mentioned, Orquesta Broadway is led and was founded by another popular five-key flute player from Cuba named Eddy Zervigon. So in all my despair, I was happy to know that Eddy Zervigon and Orquesta Broadway were still on the scene, dishing out exceptionally good music, and singlehandedly keeping charanga and the Cuban flute playing style on the Latin music radar screen against some tough odds.

Earlier, Eddy Zervigon and Orquesta Broadway exploded onto the Latin music scene with several popular recordings. "El Dengue," "Mi Socio," and "Como Camina Maria" were only a few. I had their first two albums, but I could never find where they played even though I lived only ten blocks from Eddy. I did know how good they are, and I was well aware of Eddy's command of the five-key flute, but until that time I'd never seen him play in person.

I arrived even earlier than usual on the night of Orquesta Broadway's Palladium debut performance. Once inside, it felt as if an invisible hand had picked me up and placed me at the front of the stage. It was like de-ja vu for me, and much like when I saw Johnny Pacheco play for the first time at my prom. Given the tough time I'd been having with the changes taking place with Latin music, I was thrilled about getting a chance to see another five-key flute icon in action for the first time. After scanning the group of musicians gathered on the stage, I finally spotted Eddy Zervigon. He stood with his flute tucked under his arm while he untangled a sound cable. Eddy Zervigon is a very explosive and energetic flute player, and while listening to him on his recordings, I didn't think it was possible to do the things I heard him doing. Despite that fact, I knew that I was finally going to get a chance to see it all, firsthand, at the Palladium that night. I stood at the front of the stage and watched the musicians as they tuned up and prepared for their first set. Much more familiar with the strength, range, and timbre of the compelling five-key flute's sound, I could almost hear its distinct sound ringing out in the Palladium Ballroom before Eddy started to play. While warming up, Eddy blasted one or two very high notes that rang out and seemed to hang in mid-air several seconds longer than usual. To me, they were very pleasing warning shots of things to come. Then along with that, it made a clear statement to me of how good he is and how forceful the relatively small instrument is, too.

Seeing Eddy Zervigon in person for the first time, he looked like a pretty serious guy to me. He wasn't talking, laughing, or joking around at all, he appeared to be all business. He looked like a boxer getting ready to step into a boxing ring. So for that reason, I didn't say anything to him, as I normally would have done. Nevertheless, I was still happy to know that there was still at least one five-key flute player on the NYC Latin music scene for me to learn from and keep me inspired.

When all of the musicians were in place and ready to play, I saw Eddy crouch down slightly to cue the band into their first song by tapping his foot on the floor of the stage. As soon as the music started, it was clear that Orquesta Broadway has a sound that is just as compelling as what I had always heard on their recordings. Hearing them live and in person for the first time, I was able to get a feel for their musical output even more. Their sound shot out from the stage and filled the ballroom as the dancers quickly took to the dance floor. Just as I'd done at the Americana Hotel, I didn't dance the entire night. Instead, I stood at the front of the stage in amazement as I watched Eddy take complete command of the flute, the band, the dancers, and the Palladium ballroom. He was all over the instrument, and he unleashed a hail of licks and phrases for the blissful crowd as his violin players made their instruments sing out beautifully from the other side of the stage. Along with his seemingly endless supply of flute licks, I was taken by his very percussive playing style. He played forcefully, and he was able to reach up, effortlessly, to hit notes that were at the very top end of the instrument's range. Then with each note, he seemed to turn his flute into a conga drum as he executed his solos percussively, convincingly, and flawlessly. I watched his fingers fly up and down as they covered holes and pressed keys in a swift, smooth, systematic, and highly coordinated dance of their own. This added even more excitement to everything for me. Additionally, it appeared as if he had an extra pair of lungs, and an air supply that made it possible for him to do whatever he wanted to with the instrument on one deep breath of air.

As far as I was concerned, Eddy Zervigon had taken Cuban flute playing to another level. When the dance ended, just as it happened after I saw Johnny Pacheco play for the first time, I was inspired again; and for the next few days the sound of Eddy's flute continued to resonate clearly and pleasantly in my head. The experience was a very good one for me in every way and was the perfect antidote for the Cuban-flute and charanga withdrawal pains I'd been suffering.

Over the years, I regretted not talking to Eddy that night, because I did not see him play again until sixteen years later. Then, lo and behold, some seven years after that, I was lucky enough to get to know him. Now he is one of my best friends. The initial impression I had of him as being unapproachable could have not been further from the truth. He is funny, interesting, talkative, intelligent, and is an all-around-stand-up guy. Along with that, he is always willing to share his vast knowledge and expertise with anyone who seeks him out for it.

It is an interesting story of how this renowned, talented, and longtime mentor of mine became one of my best friends; but I will get to that later. Nonetheless, given the fact that the Cuban-flute playing style had not disappeared completely from the New York City Latin music scene, if I were going to be able to continue playing music, something was going to have to happen for me soon. With my two-year stint at Newark Prep coming to an end, if I were not in school for the fall of 1968, I knew that the Selective Service would be calling on me again to have a word or two about my academic status, and my availability for military service. Adding to that thought, in terms of casualties, 1968 was the worst year of the Vietnam War.

I hope that you liked what you read so far; and if so there will be more to come in Volume II

Hasta pronto! Burrell

www.ingramcontent.com/pod-product-compliance
Lightning Source LLC
Chambersburg PA
CBHW031514120626
46545CB00005B/1879